Parable Of A President

Harold H. Haak

American Association of State
Colleges and Universities

Library of Congress Cataloging in Publication Data

Haak, Harold H.
Parable of a president.

1. College presidents. 2. Universities and colleges–Administration. I. Title.
LB2341.H23 1982 378'.111 82-16459
ISBN 0-88044-067-8

Contents

Foreword

This piece had its origins in the pesterings of a colleague who refused to accept my pleas that I was too busy to write. It is based on a presentation, entitled "Up-Tight Management," that I have made through the years to classes in business, political science, organizational psychology, and social work and to groups of administrative interns, alumni, and others interested in the workings of a university.

In the presentation, I sketch out various management approaches and then discuss how these approaches relate to the university. Putting the lecture into written form presented the difficulty that I did not have an audience with which to interact. Could I come up with examples that would have the same import as our spontaneous examples? I didn't know, but decided that by telling the story of one school year in the life of a university president I would try to illustrate the conflicts within a university.

The specific characters in this narrative truly are fictional. I have even gone through the text several times to make sure that was the case. Oh, sure, here and there you can see the virtues of some person I might know, but never the follies. In the same vein I chose the common name "Jones" for the protagonist because he is, in a sense, President "Anyone"—and he is also President "No One." Jones and I have indeed shared certain common experiences, but such is the case with many of my colleagues who have persevered as university presidents.

Likewise the specific incidents are fictional. The story is told in an exaggerated manner, but that is an advantage of a narrative format. I have been free to exaggerate to illustrate a point. In so doing I have sought the level of realism that is found when a standard university tale is told and retold over coffee in the faculty dining room.

There is no Linden State University, at least not to my knowledge. Its governance arrangement and administrative structure are unlike any university with which I have been associated, purposely so. Oh, I must confess that Jones' reorganization plan is very similar to two that I have designed based on my efforts to deal with issues similar to those raised in the book. Students, in particular, have not permitted me to stop with a description of the chaos I call "up-tight management." They have wanted to know what as president of the university I sought to do about it.

I am indebted, of course, to many scholars who have provided me with insights and a framework for viewing the university and to my many colleagues over twenty years of involvement in university governance, of which two were in a faculty leadership role and thirteen in administrative positions as dean, vice president, chancellor, and president. I am especially grateful for the stimulation of the faculties of the three universities with which I have been most closely associated.

I also must thank individually Harold L. Best, who urged me to take on this project; Betsy Kielman, who provided me with editorial advice and assistance; and my wife, who has always been my greatest source of encouragement.

Chapter One

It had been an especially hard day and President Jones couldn't sleep. Every time he thought he might doze off, another flash from the day seemed to turn on the lights and it was time for a replay of the budget hearing. Three months' preparation for a thirty-minute show, he thought, and it wasn't even a particularly good show. He should have done better.

That morning Jones had come into his office early to make sure that his papers were in order and that his budget officer had run through the numbers once more on campus energy savings. Good thing he had gotten the word that Senator Foster was asking every president how many BTU's had been saved during the past year. What the devil is a BTU, he thought. He'd have to ask on the way to the state capital. The dean of graduate studies, a chemist, would be in the car and he'd know. Wouldn't he? And what would happen if Foster or some other budget committee member started asking him about the request for new data processing equipment? He could feel the panic start to set in, but then he relaxed a little when he remembered that in his briefing with the budget committee staff member he was told that questions about data processing were out of bounds in the committee hearing and would be addressed at the staff level.

He thumbed through the green soft cover book titled "Request Budget of Linden State University, 1979-80" and felt some real pride as he thought about all the improvements that had been made since last year's budget book. Using that English professor as an editor had been a smart move. Every sentence was crisp and clear; none of the social science jargon Jones had added last year could now be found. The "accomplishments" section had some real meat to it, and the "goals and objectives" for next year were consistent with the institutional role and mission statement as well as the detailed requests in each budget schedule. This year each request was also listed explicitly in its order of priority in response to the new instructions of the budget committee. Sure the dean of arts and sciences was angry that new positions for business, architecture, engineering, and nursing were placed ahead of the arts and sciences requests. And sure the librarians were angry that their lone position request stood ignominiously at the bottom. Although they all thought the university was selling its soul, he was only trying to get what he could for the benefit of the university by responding to the latest budget instructions. Not to do so may have made campus life easier the previous summer when the budget was being put together, but there would have been hell to pay in the late spring when Linden State's new appropriation was made public.

Ken Kauffman, his budget director, came rushing in just as he was set to read, for perhaps the twentieth time, the summary section of the green book. He put it aside to give Ken his full attention, but only after he groped for a more fitting title than "Request Budget." He would have liked a more original title, one that somehow captured the effort and dreams that were reflected in the straightforward narrative and columns of numbers.

"I've got those BTU numbers for last year and this year and will go over them with you on the way," Ken blurted. "Come on. We'd better get going. It would be a disaster to be late, and maybe I can pick up some information in the halls before the hearing."

Jones liked Ken and was glad he would be doing the driving. Ken was soft-spoken, open, competent, and above all deeply concerned about Linden State. He would be the only staff member sitting beside him at the hearing and would be responsible for correcting, tactfully, any error that he might make and handing him, unobtrusively, any back-up materials he might need once the hearing got underway. In that respect, he noted that Ken's stack of papers and notebooks was some three to four times thicker than his own.

The drive up to the capital was pleasant enough. The dean of graduate studies told him more about British Thermal Units than he might want to know, but the motivation was clearly to make small talk and to pass the time. The fourth passenger was Henry Schultz, the chairman of the Board of Regents for Linden State. Schultz knew enough to limit his talk to the prospects for a third consecutive win by the football team. Jones was the third president in a little more than eight years he had escorted to the budget committee hearing, and as Schultz sized him up he felt Jones was prepared enough. Jones played along with Schultz in that he recognized in the chairman the same compassion that he had had for conscientious graduate students just before their comprehensive examinations. He tried, alternately, to act natural and to act presidential without, he supposed, much success at either.

As they walked up the steps of the capitol building, Jones had one of those insights that struck him as both funny and useful. He suddenly felt a little foolish dressed in his very best suit, as if he were a kid going to church. It would be better to dress as he did on a usual day at the campus, especially since he was about to plead for a substantial salary increase for the poor faculty of Linden State. A few minutes later the thought wasn't funny. Ken had been moseying around and had been tipped that they should be prepared for a budget committee staff analysis that showed that the university had been using money that could go to the faculty to pay high salaries to the administrators. Jones decided that it was not going to be an enjoyable hearing.

After a cup of coffee and more small talk in the snack bar, they went to the committee hearing room. Their timing was good. The committee members were only starting to come in and the university group could greet them without looking as if they had been lying in wait. The budget committee had six members, three from the Senate and three from the Assembly. Since the state was dominated by the legislature and since the budget process was the primary weapon the legislature used to work its will, the budget committee was the power center of state government. Its power was enhanced by its reputation for hard work and by the reluctance of the Senate and Assembly to undo the committee's recommendations through floor action.

Each committee member had his or her own specialty areas; in the area of higher education Senator Foster and Assemblyman Haney could be expected to do most of the questioning. Foster, a successful businessman from a small town, was known for his fairness and attention to detail. He took great pride in a state college that he had brought to his district, over the objections of the State Education Commission, and always struck Jones as a person who believed that young people should be encouraged to go to college, to learn something useful, and then to contribute to their communities. Assemblyman Haney, on the other hand, always seemed most interested in higher education because he saw it as a place where a great deal of money could be saved. He was an engineer, a graduate of a good university; supposedly he had been an honors student. As a professor, Jones had often puzzled over what universities had done to make the Haneys of the world so unappreciative of the opportunities they had enjoyed. The third member of the committee who was likely to ask Jones a question was Assemblyman Barnes, whose district was served by Linden State and who had attended the university for some real estate courses.

The audience was not large and Jones recognized most of its members. They included his faculty chairman, two officers of a faculty organization, several students, and reporters from the local and student newspapers. There were also the usual staff people from the Executive Budget and Management Office and the State Education Commission. At the back of the room Jones recognized some budget people from other universities—gathering intelligence for their own hearings, he presumed.

As the committee members took their places, the committee staff passed around some papers. Chairman Schultz made some pleasant remarks about Linden State, which were well received, introduced Jones, and then joined the audience. Jones was on. Because this was his second hearing, he thought he knew what was expected of him, so he asked the committee to turn to the summary section of the green book.

He started to go over Linden State's role and mission statement and its relation to its program goals and accomplishments when he was interrupted by Senator Foster. "Could you be brief, President Jones? We only have half an hour because we senators are needed on the floor at 10:30 for an important vote." Jones stumbled about as best he could, cutting still shorter an already succinct five-page summary of his beloved green book, when he was rescued by Assemblyman Haney, who said, "President Jones, we have all had copies of your budget request made available to us, and I assure you we all know how to read. I'd like to make the best use of our time by getting right to some questions."

Haney noted that Linden State's top priority was to increase faculty salaries. Why then had it last year not given the faculty all the possible salary money that the legislature had made available? More specifically, he had noted from his (that is, the staff's) analysis of the budget book that Linden State had transferred money from the faculty line, that could have gone to increasing salaries, to its operating expense line. It appeared to him that as president of the university Jones was responsible for compounding the very salary problem that he now wanted the legislature to rectify with still more money.

The budget committee, of course, had itself contributed greatly to the situation about which they now complained. They had required a separate line for paying the faculty, and Haney himself would have violently objected if Linden State had ended the year with a greater expenditure for salaries than the legislature intended. Given the rules of the state budget process, Linden State started with a plan to spend all of the salary dollars on the faculty, but there were always some unexpected vacancies that led to salary savings that were then transferred to other lines.

Jones knew that Haney understood as well as he the answer to the question, and he also knew that the answer he gave sounded obscure and unconvincing to the faculty and the reporters whose faces he couldn't see behind him. Well, Ken could follow up with the faculty representatives and the press. It would be all right.

Next, Haney asked a committee staff member to give Jones a copy of a comparative analysis he had done of Linden State's administrative salaries. The analysis indicated that administrative salaries were significantly above the averages of the comparison group. "Why are you spending so much salary money on administrators when that money should go to the faculty?" Haney demanded.

It took little effort to point out that an inappropriate comparison group had been used. The committee staff had lumped Linden State together with small state colleges that offered no graduate or professional programs.

By this time Senator Foster had had enough and shifted the discussion to the physical plant section of the green book. Jones thought that Foster was pleased when, in response to a question, he nonchalantly and unhesitatingly cited the BTU's Linden State had saved through its energy conservation program.

Assemblyman Barnes chimed in with a remark that Linden State's enrollments were higher than expected last year. Linden State was a popular institution that served the people of the state well. Haney could not resist commenting that the campus had shown its ability to handle the extra students with the number of faculty and staff that it had last year and certainly, in view of the state's tight fiscal situation, it could do it again without additional employees.

And so twenty-five minutes had flown by when Senator Foster asked if any member of the audience wished to address the committee. A young man identified himself as a Linden State business student and complained that he could not enroll in several business classes because they were oversubscribed. Linden State needed the added faculty that had been requested.

Senator Foster looked through several papers, found what he wanted, and paused as he appeared to make some mental calculations. He responded to the student but looked directly at Jones. The legislature had given the campus the number of positions it deserved but the campus had misallocated them. There were too few students and too many faculty in the arts and sciences. That was the basic cause of the difficulties faced by the business students.

"President Jones," Haney chimed in, "you're responsible for the spending of millions of dollars of state tax money. We expect you to spend those dollars to meet this state's, and this legislature's commitment to our young people, not to make your own life easier."

"I would like to underscore the concern expressed by the student," added Barnes. "I faced the same problem a number of years ago when I took courses in the Linden State School of Business. Now, President Jones, you have made clear in your request budget that the first new positions you receive should go to the business department. We'll expect you to do just that."

At this point a buzzer rang. It was time for the senators to rush to the floor and the hearing was quickly concluded.

The conversation on the way back to Linden State was subdued. Jones was too busy coping with his internal irritation with the committee, and anger with himself for not doing better, to say much. He felt that he had been pretty badly beaten up, and the worst part was that the beating took place in front of an audience. His mind drifted back to the time that a little kid in the sixth grade gave him a bloody nose in front of his buddies.

He wondered what the graduate dean was thinking. Maybe that the day had been a waste of his time. Jones had wanted him along because they had anticipated some technical questions concerning indirect cost recoveries resulting from research programs, but the topic had never come up. More probably, he found the spectacle interesting and he was quiet now because he didn't know what to say.

Finally Ken started up a conversation. "Smythe from the committee staff gave me seven follow-up questions that I'll get right to work on. I'll also make it a point to drop by the faculty senate office to make sure that the faculty leadership gets the word on salary savings and administrative salaries. By the way, Smythe thought you did pretty well at the hearing."

"Yes, that was Barnes' impression," Henry Schultz added. "We chatted a bit right after the hearing. He brought up the problems of the business school again, so you'd better expect some follow-up from his office and I'm sure we'll want to discuss the topic some more at the next board meeting."

"I've been going to these hearings for some years now," he continued, "and I always feel better when the committee acts a little tough. It means that they've read the materials and they're thinking about giving us some more money."

Jones knew that Ken and Schultz would tell the truth, perhaps in this case somewhat selectively to make him feel better, so he relaxed a little and helped the conversation turn to small talk that would make the trip go faster.

When Jones got back to Linden State he went directly to his office. Fortunately, the office staff already knew him well enough not to say much, and he was able quickly to close the door and be by himself.

He supposed he had better return a few of those calls. He'd get them off his back and then go home.

The first call was to Dick Peters, a local banker and president of the boosters' club. Jones liked Dick. He was direct, supportive, and consistent. Dick had played guard on Linden State's last great football team, in '48, and was commonly viewed as an ex-jock, but Jones knew that he had given Linden State money to help handicapped students as well as tailbacks. He remembered asking himself, as the phone rang, if football guards from Dick's era had a common personality type. They were always small for playing in the line, and he remembered how they used to pull out and do the blocking ahead of the runner on those end sweeps and off-tackle plays.

"Dick? Hubert Jones here. I had a note to call you."

"Thank you for calling right back, Hubert. I know you're very busy, so let me get right to the point. A few of us have been discussing Linden State's athletics program. It's great for the town and the university, and you know we want to do what we can to help you with it. Now, the way we see it is that it's really going to go only with your leadership and we've come upon a way to improve the general situation. We'd like the athletics director to report directly to you. That way he wouldn't get bogged down in that bureaucracy you run at the college and the program would have the kind of priority and visibility it needs. Given it some thought, would you? You could make the move part of that university reorganization plan you discussed with me at Rotary last Thursday."

He promised Dick that he would give the matter careful consideration and went on to the next call, one from Martha Davis, a new member of the Board of Regents.

"Hi, Martha. Hubert Jones returning your call."

"Hubert, thank you for calling." They went through an awkward ten-minute conversation about the budget committee hearing and other matters before Martha Davis brought out her real concern. "Linden State, though, has one area where it needs to get its act together and that's in affirmative action. We don't have the number of minority students we should have, and the women and minority staff members on the campus just aren't treated fairly. They've opened up to me about it many times, and this is one area where I, as a new board member, want to see if I can be of help. Hubert, we're not going to get anyplace until the whole campus sees some signs from the board and from you that we're serious about the matter, that affirmative action is one of our top priorities. We've got to go beyond policy statements and affirmative action plans and do some things that are more dramatic. For one thing, I would like to see the affirmative action director report directly to you in that new reorganization plan when it is presented to the board for its review. Then I've got some other ideas as to how we as the board can show our commitment. In particular, I'm talking to Regent Schultz about our budget for women's sports. It's a shame that we're spending so much on football and ignoring our other institutional responsibilities. By the way, I need some information about the money we spend on various sports. Oh, Hubert, I have a long distance call coming in."

They agreed he would call her the next day to continue the conversation. He wanted to go home but thought it best to make one more call. The caller had been angry and refused to leave his name. Always better to get these things out of the way right away, he thought, as the phone rang.

"This is President Jones from Linden State returning your call. Could I help you?"

"I hope so. I'm so damn mad at you guys at the university that I can hardly think straight. I've spent the whole day trying to get my registration straightened out. One of my transcripts didn't come and now they tell me I won't get credit for the courses I'm in. You guys may be able to push around the younger students, but some of us have been around for a while. I told that smart-aleck kid in admissions that I was going right to the top for an answer."

Well, Jones thought, the caller's gone to the top seeking an answer, but frankly "the top" didn't even understand the question. Like most people, the caller settled down, and Jones was able to convince him that it was best for him to see the dean of students. The dean of students gets an "A" at Linden State, Jones felt, in that he judged the effectiveness of staff members by whether the people he sent to them ended up back at his door. When people went to the dean of students with a problem, they seemed to disappear. "I wonder how he does it?" he asked himself.

It was time to go home and he was grateful that the campus was largely deserted. He didn't want to talk to anyone.

Jones finally faced squarely the fact that it would be some time before he could go to sleep. He knew that in a few days the keen frustration that he felt would become first distant and then forgotten as he became preoccupied with new deadlines, issues, and demands. As for now, he had some ideas that he wanted to jot down before they were forgotten and he might as well get up. When he was teaching he used to get some of his best work done in these late hours when there were no interruptions from the kids.

The budget committee hearing, he wrote after he poured his first cup of coffee, was set up to enhance the power and purposes of the committee's members–not his. That was simple lesson number one. It all started with the instructions for preparing the green budget request book. First there was the statutory language establishing Linden State; next the role and mission statement approved by the State Education Commission, the legislature's agent; and only then Linden State's own goals and priorities. These provided the context in which specific requests were made. A given in the arrangement was that the budget committee held the high ground at the start of any battle at the hearing.

The green book presented an unambiguous picture of the university that hid the pain and struggles that went into its development. Jones as president was expected to show a personal mastery of all its details, and he was expected to deliver clear, crisp answers to questions that denied the university's complexity. To reinforce this expectation, only his budget officer, Ken, was permitted to sit beside him. Jones had crammed diligently to create the impression that he indeed was on top of things, firmly in control of detail, and thinking back over the hearing he took some pleasure in recalling that he had not had to rely upon Ken to respond to a question.

By treating Jones as if he were personally in control of all of the university's activities, the legislators sought to maximize their own influence. It was an old tactic in government. Hold the agency director's feet to the fire and through him exercise control downward through the organization. In fact, the budget committee had treated him pretty much as they did the heads of state bureaus and departments. Likening the university to other governmental agencies would be anathema to Jones' colleagues, but that seemed to be the way the legislators saw it.

It also became clearer to Jones why committee members often seemed to ask questions to which they knew the answers. In part, he had participated in a ritual in which he played the part of the lamb. The people's elected representatives, their legislators, were flexing their muscles and demonstrating their complete authority and mastery over the appointed agency head. He wished he could dismiss the whole affair as a ritual, but he couldn't. The stakes—in terms of money for Linden State—were potentially too high.

The budget committee members were not the only ones who expected him to be firmly in charge of the university, to be "the boss." In those phone conversations today, Dick

Peters and Martha Davis, both of whom wanted particular programs to report directly to him, seemed to share that view. Assign responsibility for a program directly to him and its high priority in the university was assured. And then there was the irate caller that Jones had talked to at the close of the day. He knew how the world operated—and thus went directly to the top.

In fact, when most people in our society think about organizations, Jones continued to write, they seem to have in mind a model in which there is a single person directing everything from the top. It was like scientific management's organizational model. As he remembered it, the scientific management school started with the principle of the division of labor into simple tasks. Workers would be expected to accomplish these tasks quickly and repetitively. Someone would have to organize and direct these efforts, and that job would fall to a single boss. "Unity of command" he thought they called it. Since one person could supervise effectively only a limited number of persons ("span of control" wasn't it called), but those persons in turn could supervise still others, the whole organization took on the appearance of a pyramid or triangle.

He then sketched out a triangle, and envisioned a stern person in charge, issuing orders to the workers at the bottom through a chain of command.

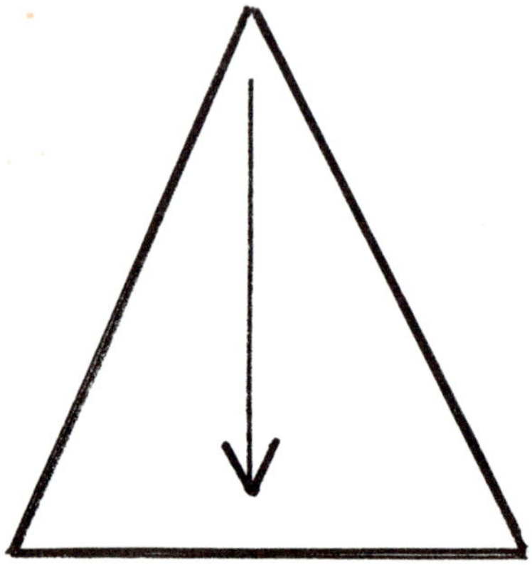

"TOP-DOWN" MANAGEMENT

Jones was growing tired and his mind drifted back to a regents' meeting that he had attended in 1968 when he had been a faculty member. He had liked the president who was then being grilled unmercifully by the governor's new appointees to the board. Everyone knew there would be trouble ahead when one of the regents brought out a copy of the student newspaper, the one with the nudes on the front page and the generous spattering of four-letter words. How did the president account for this? Who was responsible? The behavior had to stop. It belittled the dignity of the university, destroyed public trust, and indicated to the people of the state that the university was out of control. The president said he would take the matter up with the editorial board responsible for the newspaper and began extolling the virtues of a free press. ("We hired you to run the campus. You're responsible.") The new board members hadn't really hired him, but they soon played a central role in ousting him and selecting his successor. Now that Jones himself was a president, he didn't know how he would have handled the situation and felt even more empathy for his departed colleague.

He would go back to bed. Some other time he would look over what he had written to see if it still made any sense.

Chapter Two

A week had passed since the debacle with the legislative budget committee. Ken had handled the concerns with the faculty leadership and the reporters, and both the student and community newspapers presented as clear a picture as they could of the salary savings issue. To his pleasant surprise, Jones found that the faculty's reaction focused on the comparison group the committee staff had used for its analysis of administrative salaries. "How could they lump us together with those state colleges! They just don't appreciate that Linden State is now a full-fledged university." Jones knew that there would be a day of reckoning on the positions for business, but that issue could be faced in the spring when the legislature approved the final budget and Linden State had some hard figures. Jones was also surprised that the budget committee staff had asked Ken for still more information on energy savings; Senator Foster was apparently determined to keep up the pressure.

The week had passed easily, or at least it seemed so. Linden State won its fourth straight on the gridiron, an easy victory that brought great joy to the enthusiasts and some boredom to those more marginally interested in football. The drama department's play was excellent and no one from the community had hassled him about the nudity scene. Personally, Jones had found the scene amusing, but he had quickly become concerned about the community's reaction when, at the close of the intermission, he happened to overhear the negative remarks of the elderly couple sitting in front of him. His talk before the Exchange Club went well. He had dispensed with the prepared text and formality that characterized his speeches in his first year. His new confidence showed through and he was better able to adjust his remarks to the interests of particular audiences.

Jones had especially enjoyed the all-day planning retreat on general education attended by the deans and the faculty leaders. He still clung to the vision of the president as the leader of the faculty, but his opportunities to discuss educational issues were becoming more and more limited. Sometimes he wondered if he should have remained a dean, but he didn't wonder for long. Both Linden State and his previous institution had had strong faculty senates. Jones remembered too well how he felt moving from his faculty leadership role to the deanship. He had gone from a position where he was able to exert what he considered to be great influence on universitywide policy issues to a middle management position that held little interest for him. "It's up or out for me," he told his wife after he had asked a colleague to nominate him for several vice presidencies and two presidencies, including that of Linden State.

Sure Jones was a little tired—the four nights out after the strenuous preparation for the budget committee hearing, the string of committee meetings, and the usual hassles—but all in all it had been a busy and productive week.

He tried not to think much about the budget committee hearing. He had to put the experience behind him and move onto other things. Still, inwardly he was disturbed and annoyed. As he pulled together some papers for his meeting with the two vice presidents, he thought to himself that perhaps his attitudes had been too influenced by his experiences as a faculty member. Maybe he really should act more like the boss.

The meeting with the two vice presidents started out well enough. Jones went through a quick summary of the budget committee hearing and speculated about what it meant in terms of money for Linden State. The two vice presidents had been around long enough to know that they shouldn't ask too many questions about the hearing itself. Jones realized that he appreciated the fact that the group always tried to be mutually supportive and merciful toward whoever had recently taken a beating.

The vice president for academic affairs reported on the progress being made on redoing the institutional master plan for the State Education Commission, on developing a new general education program, and on the faculty senate's consideration for a new promotions procedure.

Albert Smith had been a good vice president for academic affairs and Jones was glad that he had kept him on when he became president. Of course, Smith was still smarting from the battle he had with the faculty during the tenure of the previous president, William C. Peabody. Peabody had come to Linden State from a prestigious eastern university and had set out to upgrade the faculty, a goal consistent with Linden State's relatively recently acquired role as a university. Consequently Smith had been given the task of being much tougher on tenure and promotions decisions, especially when it came to publications standards. Now the faculty was busy redoing the promotions procedure to make sure that Smith's power over outcomes would be greatly limited. The draft Smith had in front of him had many new provisions for the giving of reasons, for referral back to lower levels when changes were contemplated, and for explicit rank-order listings by the University Board on Promotions.

Jones let Smith talk for some time because he knew the vice president was vexed. It was important that they take time out to help one another. Jones also knew that he, himself, was no longer very interested in faculty procedures. What would have preoccupied him as a faculty member was now distant from his interests. Of course, he knew that the problem Smith was outlining would most likely come back to haunt him. Unless some agreement was reached, Jones recognized that eventually the faculty senate would force him to choose between supporting his vice president and upholding the will of the faculty expressed legitimately through its faculty senate. Jones listened more closely to Smith, let him finish, and decided that they would have to discuss the topic at a future meeting when he felt more up to it.

It was then the turn of Bob Bashford, the vice president for business affairs. Bashford had been with the university for twenty-seven years and had come up through the ranks. He was a competent administrator who had demonstrated a remarkable tolerance for the idiosyncracies of the many vice presidents for academic affairs and presidents with whom he had worked.

Bashford correctly sized up the moods of his colleagues, reported on the progress being made in installing the new computer, and said everything else he had could wait.

The consequence of Bashford's short report was that the group had some fifteen minutes left before Jones' next appointment, so Jones asked, "Bob, do you have some ideas as to how we can better ourselves in terms of energy savings? As you know, Senator Foster is not letting up."

"Sure," Bob answered. "We have several ideas that I've been anxious to put into action. I'm not sure how well they'd be accepted on campus, but they would all help our position."

"What do you have in mind, Bob?"

"Well, first of all, as you know we have that new computerized control system that keeps all the building temperatures at their optimum levels in terms of energy usage, especially during the critical peak hours. The only problem is that the faculty and the secretaries keep opening their windows. In comes the outside air, boom—there go the thermostats, and up go our energy costs. What we really ought to do is to have the guts to close those windows permanently so that they can't be opened by everybody who feels a little bit of discomfort or who wants to smoke in the classrooms. We should have done it several years ago."

"Well, why haven't we?"

"I don't know quite how to say it, but I just didn't think I'd get the backing when the faculty and the staff start screaming."

Jones appreciated Bashford's honesty, but his internal fight mechanisms also sensed a challenge and he wanted to strike back. Besides, maybe he *was* too academic and should assert himself more often as the boss. Without his customary caution, Jones took a fix on Bashford and said, "Well, Bob, if it's the right thing to do in your judgment, let's go do it."

"Since we've jumped the first hurdle, let me go over some other plans we've had in mind," Bashford continued. "We've talked to the Campus Planning Committee about a plan to encourage the use of bicycles on campus by closing the center of the campus to cars. We'd also get a lot better usage out of those new perimeter parking lots that go unused while people yell about a parking problem. Campus Planning likes the idea. They've also supported our proposal to subsidize a van, or minibus, serving the dormitories on the south end of campus. We know that quite a few kids drive their cars from there to the center of campus and think that we could help cut down on their use of fuel by gas guzzlers if we provided them with an alternative. We'd also have a safer campus with less traffic. We could pay for the van out of parking ticket revenues."

"The other thing we ought to do," Bashford added, "is to close down the buildings between semesters. Pitifully few people are on campus at the time, and we could save some real fuel dollars by not having to heat the buildings in the dead of winter. Wow, those fuel bills are eating us alive. It used to be that we counted on some flexibility in the utilities budget to get us through some tight fiscal situations. Now we have to shuffle other money into utilities and we're getting ourselves into a lot of trouble down the road."

Jones wasn't much interested in the business affairs of the campus and had a lot of confidence in Bashford. Maybe what was needed was to turn Bashford loose. Give him some encouragement and some backing. He looked at his watch and saw it was nearly time for his next appointment.

"Bob, I'd like you to follow through on your ideas. You're the expert on these things." Jones tried to look assertive as he sent Bashford on his way. It would take him some time to be comfortable in his new role as the boss. He hoped that the older and more experienced Bob Bashford didn't sense his own lack of confidence.

A few days later Bashford called to tell Jones the physical plant was undertaking the fixing of the windows and that campus security was setting up signs to notify people of the changes that would take place in campus traffic and parking patterns. The student newspaper had gotten wind of the changes and Bashford would be interviewed tomorrow. He wondered if Jones would like him to arrange an interview with the community newspaper. There might be a lot of community interest in what the campus was doing to save on energy.

Jones followed his instincts and said he thought it would be premature to contact the outside press. He also noted to himself that Bashford seemed to be in a good mood. There was new zest and even zeal in his voice. For just a moment the thought occurred to him that perhaps there was a little too much zeal.

The following Monday Jones was uncomfortable as he drove onto the campus. That special parking permit that had been placed on the right hand corner of his windshield seemed to obscure his vision. It was made necessary, of course, because of the new parking and traffic regulations. Without it he soon would not be able to get to his own parking space by the Administration Building near the center of campus. The signs indicating the soon-to-be-enforced traffic flow and parking regulations were everywhere. No one could complain about inadequate notice, he thought to himself. As he entered the parking lot by the Administration Building, he noticed that already a security officer was letting by only those automobiles that had the new parking sticker. He couldn't remember who all had one. He thought he'd better tell Bashford to limit their number sharply or there might be a negative reaction about special privileges. Who should get them? He, the two vice presidents, and the deans whose offices were in the Administration Building. That's all. Well, he would have to make sure that Jean, his administrative assistant, had one. He caught his mind wandering in time to slam on the brakes before he collided with two undergraduates, who, arm in arm and obviously oblivious to his car, were making the trek across the parking lot to get from the Humanities Building to the Business Building. Too bad there's not more traffic between those two buildings, he thought. At least the new traffic rules would cut down on the possibility that Linden State would tragically eliminate some of what there was.

As he took the short walk from his parking place to the Administration Building, Jones was developing a feeling that he was in trouble. Then the secretary from the graduate office omitted her usual friendly hello when they passed one another at the entrance. The nod was polite, and if he hadn't always enjoyed her cheerful attitude, he might not have noticed the absence of verbal communication. He was glad that he had stressed at the staff orientation the importance of staff attitudes on campus morale and image. Linden State had a good staff and they were known throughout the community for their helpful attitude. That call he had received the other day from the disgruntled older student was, fortunately, the exception. Where was the staff? He noticed that the hallways of the Administration Building seemed rather empty even though it was nine o'clock.

When he came into his own suite of offices, he noticed that the secretaries were all very busy. Only Esther looked up and said, "Good morning, Dr. Jones."

He came into Jean's office. She was involved in an animated conversation. "I'll have him call you as soon as he comes in. . . . Look, I said I would have him call you. Just hold tight. I'll talk to him, so hope for the best."

"Sorry I didn't call to tell you I'd be a little late," Jones said. "I was glad to see no one waiting in the outer office. I didn't remember the time of my first appointment. It was a big night last night. Big turnout for the football banquet, and the coach went over the accomplishments of every player. It pays to be ten-and-one for the season. Some of the boosters are talking about raising the money to fix up the stadium."

"Dr. Jones, I have to talk to you about something really important," Jean interrupted. "That was the seventh phone call I've gotten in the last forty-five minutes. Sorry if I seemed sharp with the caller but my patience is wearing a little thin. We've got a problem. The gals in the graduate office hit me with it at 7:30 this morning over coffee. Two faculty members from Communicative Disorders even talked to me about it, and they haven't talked to anyone from this building since Smith turned down the department chairman for promotion."

"What is it?" Jones asked, looking down at the stack of phone calls he was supposed to return, a stack that wasn't there on Saturday morning when he had sneaked in to get caught up on his paperwork.

Jean settled down quickly and related the events of the morning. As she did so, Jones listened attentively. It wasn't like Jean to lose her cool so it must be something important. It seemed that over the weekend physical plant staff had started to screw down the windows so they couldn't be opened. They had begun in the old Education Building with the offices of the faculty in Communicative Disorders and then moved on to the Administration Building. Bashford's offices and the Graduate Office had been hit. Some of the phone calls had been from Bashford's own offices.

The callers expressed their outrage in various ways, denied opening their windows on either hot or cold days, and claimed their constitutional right to fresh air. Unless Jones took quick action, Jean advised, there would be a first class revolt. At eight o'clock workers from the physical plant had even come to the President's Office, and Jean had told them to hold everything.

Jones made one call—to Bashford—and suggested that the effort to fasten down the windows go no further. Bashford agreed and Jones asked Jean to give him only the calls that didn't relate to the Monday morning crisis. Would she handle the others? The two calls he returned went quickly, and Jones found himself irritated that he didn't have some pressing paperwork to occupy his attention.

A few days later Jones met with the vice president for academic affairs and with dean of students Farber. They asked if he would be willing to meet with the student affairs staff. The staff was especially worked up about the new campus plan for traffic and parking. Jones asked why Smith and Farber couldn't handle the problem themselves, and they indicated that they had no authority over the particular matter that concerned the staff and that they were not well informed about the topic.

"Well, why not have Bashford meet with them?" Jones asked.

Smith's explanation was a long one. It seemed that the student affairs people were very sensitive about Bashford and the business affairs office. Former President Peabody had proposed that student affairs move from Smith's area to Bashford's and there was an impression that the proposal came about at Bashford's instigation. The student affairs people were very concerned about their image in the university and their relationship with the faculty. In fact, the counselors and some of the other professionals thought they should be considered members of the faculty. The campaign to stay under Smith was successful, but there were still some old wounds. The whole thing would go so much better if the president met with the group, not Bashford; Smith and Farber would be there to help in every way they could.

In addition, the dean noted, the group from admissions and records wanted to discuss with the president a proposed new procedure for admitting older students that they understood was of interest to him.

Although he was not entirely sure why, Jones agreed to meet with the student affairs staff that Thursday afternoon.

On Thursday afternoon Jones and Smith rushed from their meeting with the faculty executive committee to Old Main, which housed the bulk of the student affairs staff. Neither one of them was in a good mood. Smith had become anxious about some demands the faculty were pressing in the new promotions procedure, and he had become angry about some remarks made by faculty members in Communicative Disorders. Jones was irritated because the discussion revolved around a few phrases whose full intent he couldn't quite grasp. It didn't help matters that he remembered writing into a personnel document similar phrases when he was the chairman of a faculty personnel committee. He wished he could remember what he had then had in mind.

Old Main was never designed to house a student affairs staff, but the uses to which the space had been put were a testimony to ingenuity. Somehow they had even managed to keep free one of Linden State's first classrooms for use as a conference room that would accommodate most of the staff at one time.

How had they managed to get that by Bashford, Jones wondered to himself.

Jones knew there was trouble as soon as he came into the room. It was overcrowded. All the chairs around the long conference table were filled. Other chairs, also taken, formed an outer circle around the table. Jones looked at the circular pattern and assumed that the counselors had something to do with setting up the room. A few people stood at the back of the room.

A place was made for Jones and Smith at the head of the conference table, and chairs were brought in for those who were standing. Farber, as dean of students, welcomed the president and the vice president. All were asked to introduce themselves. The purpose of the meeting was solemnly stated. Jones thanked the student affairs staff for their contributions to the university, expressed his pleasure for the opportunity to meet with them, and explained as best he could the rationale behind the new traffic and parking rules. He went on to cite the national urgency to save energy and thought to himself that he had stated the case with some eloquence.

The discussion that followed was polite and to the point. The concerns went far beyond the student affairs staff, but perhaps they were the first to express them because Old Main was the most distant building from the outlying parking areas and because the dean had just instituted new evening hours to provide better service to the part-time and nontraditional evening students. People from the community were afraid to come on the campus at night and certainly would be even more discouraged if they couldn't use the close-in parking spaces. The women staff members were very concerned about walking through the campus to the outlying areas at night. Rape was an everpresent danger and the university had to be more sensitive to the needs of its women employees. Regent Davis had met with the women's caucus on campus and was very sensitive to staff members' concerns.

Some of the proposed changes were good, especially those that would make bicycling safer for students. The staff, however, felt they had some other ideas that were even better and wished that the administration had taken the time to consult with them before making such arbitrary changes. They wanted to be helpful. They wanted to get along with the administration. They felt good will toward President Jones and appreciated his willingness to meet with them. What was needed was a faculty-student-staff task force to study the whole matter and to come up with recommendations to the president. The present plan should not be implemented.

Jones was ready to concede after the first half hour. He even took well the reference to administrative preferential treatment and elitism built into the parking plan. At least, he thought to himself, if he scotched the whole thing quickly he wouldn't have to consider parking out in the boondocks himself.

"I think you have done a very good job of expressing some things that we hadn't thought about," Jones said. "Vice President Smith and I will meet with Vice President Bashford and we'll look at the idea of setting up a task force to review the whole matter. I'm sure we can work it all out."

"President Jones?" The voice was that of a counselor who was obviously a leader in the group and who had made a great deal of sense in his earlier remarks. "I think we have a larger problem at Linden State, one that this whole thing has brought to everyone's attention. The faculty of the university has its senate, and the students have student government. We staff members don't have a way to participate in the development of university policies that affect us. I think that the university would benefit a great deal from more participation by the staff. In this case and others, things would go a lot more smoothly if the staff had a voice in developing policies and not be put in the position of seeking to overturn what we view to be arbitrary actions that come down from the top. Like you, we want Linden State to be even better. There's a lot of talent in this room and elsewhere in the university that's not being tapped. What I have in mind, Dr. Jones, is a staff council representing staff throughout the university. Something like the faculty senate. A few of us have been working on the idea and we have a draft constitution that we would like to share with you. What's your reaction to the idea?"

"Frankly I've been very impressed by this meeting and your suggestions," Jones replied. "I've always felt that Linden State has an excellent staff and your idea may provide us with a way to make still better use of the talent in the staff and to prevent the kinds of misunderstandings that led to this meeting."

Vice President Smith and Dean Farber added their agreement that the idea had great promise, and Jones indicated that they and Vice President Bashford would give it careful consideration.

When Jones got back to his office he was feeling better about himself. He called Bashford and went over the meeting, emphasizing that the student affairs staff thought that the new traffic and parking plan had many good points about it. However, he asked Bashford to hold up any further implementation until after a staff-student-faculty task force had been able to review the whole matter. He closed the conversation by asking Bashford and the personnel officer to get together with a counselor in student affairs—Farber would have the name—and set in motion the formation of staff council. When Jones hung up, he reflected that Bashford would likely feel some resentment toward him and he was thankful that Bashford had developed so much tolerance for the ways that the university operated.

Jones had heard that there was almost no ridership on the new van and that Bashford was thinking about canceling the pilot program. He would underscore the value of the experiment and urge Bashford to keep it up. That might make Bashford feel better, but he doubted it.

On his way out, Jean gave hime an earlier message from Bashford. A delegation from the support staff had visited him concerning a rumor that they had heard to the effect that the campus would close down over the winter recess and employees would be required to take leave. If so, the staff employee organization planned to sue Linden State. Bashford, Jean explained, had told them that the idea had been under consideration but had been dropped. He trusted that the president would agree with what he had done.

As soon as Jones came home he went to his desk, found the notes he had made after the budget committee hearing, and immediately drew a new triangle; he drew an arrow from the bottom to the top. "Bottoms-up management," that was it.

He remembered reading a book with that phrase in its title when he was a master's degree student.

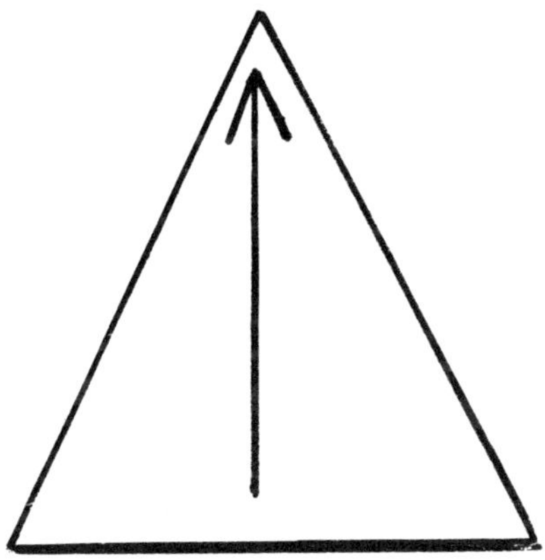

"BOTTOMS-UP" MANAGEMENT

Jones was exhilarated. He had rediscovered for himself, in his own experience, what the scientific management researchers had found at the Hawthorne plant of the Western Electric Company. There was more to an organization than its formal structure, he wrote. Informal organization was important. People were important. They would work harder and contribute more when they had an opportunity to participate and to grow in their jobs. Work should not be just assigned to them; they should participate in the development of policies that affected them. Happy employees are better employees. That was it and Jones was sure it was also true of bosses.

He should not have played the boss. It wasn't natural to him. He himself should have proposed the formation of a staff council like the faculty senate to which he was accustomed.

Jones felt rushed. His wife was urging him to get ready for the reception they would be attending for the visiting professor from England. They would be late. They musn't be late because they had to stay a while and still be at the Schultz's by 7:30 for dinner. He tucked his papers back in the desk drawer. He wished he had more time to write out his insights. He would come back to the notes some other time, but he knew they would no longer look brilliant, most of all to him.

At the Schultz's he discussed his need to reform his ways and to treat Linden State's staff with the full dignity they deserved. The others listened politely but were not very interested. He felt somewhat uncomfortable himself when he was expressing his disappointment that the idea of a staff council had not come from him. For some reason it seemed more appropriate, in the midst of his monologue, that the suggestion had come from the counselor. Unfortunately, or fortunately, Schultz did not give him the opportunity to think the matter through clearly. He asserted his authority as the chairman of the board to change the topic to the visiting professor's views on the status of the British economy and what the experience might augur for the United States. "Sorry to cut you short, Hubert, but I appear to be the only one willing to do that to the illustrious president of our fine university."

Jones sulked for a while and then joined the conversation. Soon he found himself arguing for a tight monetary policy and a return to the gold standard. He knew little about economics, but Schultz had been right. Everyone was happy participating in an open-ended discussion. He shouldn't so dominate conversations. He should listen more. A half hour later the discussion had become a glorious argument that he really enjoyed. It was a great evening.

Chapter Three

Jones was reading his mail before his meeting with Smith to go over their presentation on academic planning before the State Education Commission. He had made his quick sort and a big stack went directly into the out basket. In the case of those long memoranda from the Commission and other state agencies, he had become comfortable with the procedure whereby Jean would read through the materials carefully and if there was something he needed to know would mark the appropriate sections with a paper clip.

The first document he read carefully was an audit report marked "confidential." The state auditors had visited the campus to check on Linden State's instructional equipment record keeping and control system. The first part of the report looked routine enough. There were technical suggestions that Bashford could easily handle. Smith would not want to concern himself with those. The next section dealt with some irregularities that were more serious. In particular, faculty members were taking equipment home without properly checking it out. In one case last September, a physics professor had gone so far as to take home a minicomputer, which had never been returned. There was no record that he had even checked it out, but the department chairman had quickly come up with his name when the auditor had inquired about the missing equipment.

Jean had tacked a note onto the section. The Physics Department was very angry about the auditor's intrusion into the affairs of the department. Of course Professor Lockwood had the minicomputer at home. The department's offices were too small to let anyone work creatively at the campus. Lockwood was the faculty's leading innovator when it came to using the minicomputer for science instruction. He worked every night at home preparing new materials for his classes, that is, when he wasn't working on a paper. Not only was Lockwood an exciting and innovative instructor, but this year he had published two papers and had delivered another at a national conference.

Jean's note also related some comments Ken had made when he brought over the audit report. No doubt the report would be used by the state purchasing department in its biannual effort to bring Linden State's operations under the purview of the department, thereby in its view enhancing efficiency and economies of scale.

Jones next turned to some memoranda that obviously had not been typed by one of the secretaries. They were characterized by their poor ditto quality and the typeovers. The three of them had been paper clipped together. The first was a blistering attack on the acting dean of the School of Social Sciences, an historian, by one of his senior colleagues in history. It was addressed to the dean with copies to seven other persons, including Jones, Smith, and the chairman of the faculty senate. The second was the dean's curt, hostile reply with copies to the same persons. The third was the senior historian's response to the dean's reply.

And so it would go on, Jones thought to himself. He wondered why such memoranda were so seldom typed by the secretaries. Was it that they were written and sent off on the spur of the moment, while the blood pressure and creative energies were at a high point? Or was it that other such missives were indeed typed by secretaries who managed in their own ways to calm bruised egos and to see that there was a cooling off period after which the memos were never sent? Or maybe the authors knew intrinsically that the secretaries had more important things to type or that they shouldn't be drawn into the faculty warfare.

The School of Social Sciences was in disarray and was on its third dean in four years. The anthropologists wanted to split off from the sociologists, but had too few faculty to do so under the university's guidelines. The young economists wanted to seize control of the department from their more conservative and quantitatively oriented senior colleagues. The political scientists were resentful of the efforts of the School of Business to develop a public administration option and had temporarily dropped their efforts to oust the public administration types from their department. The geographers were smarting from what they viewed as a defeat at the hands of the geologists in the determination of the physical science requirement in the new general education package. The history department had a splinter group that wanted to join the humanities, led by the same senior faculty member who was attacking the dean. The urban planning program did not understand how it fit into the structure of the School of Social Sciences and was meeting informally with the public administration types to consider the formation of a new department, possibly in the School of Business.

Jones had been the dean of a school that included the social sciences and knew from his experience that, although he received a copy of each memorandum, he was expected to stay out of the fray. Social scientists were always confident that they could run their own affairs, in their departments, if the administration would only let them.

The resignation of the dean last September had meant that Smith had become directly involved. Following consultation with the faculty, Smith had asked a crusty senior member of the history department to fill in until a new dean could be selected through the regular search process, which meant, in effect, for the remainder of the academic year. The acting dean had a reputation for toughness. He had been the chairman of the history department some twenty years earlier and since that time had shown the good sense to avoid administrative assignments and committee work, which he disdained.

The acting dean felt that he had little to lose and set out to straighten out some of the bad practices of his colleagues. He began by rigidly enforcing office hours, travel regulations, and attendance at school faculty meetings. He had sniffed out three junior faculty members who had not declared their involvement in outside consulting activities and had mercilessly raked them over the coals, to the great irritation of their department chairmen who resented his interference. Currently he was after faculty members who did not plan to attend commencement and he was developing a rather elaborate plan to ensure that all final examinations were given during the official final examination period.

Jones felt great empathy for his social science colleagues and could identify with the harsh sentiments expressed in the memoranda sent to the acting dean. He was a disaster. Good thing the auditors didn't come upon him; they would have recommended him for an efficiency award. Although Jones found the whole fiasco somewhat amusing, he knew Smith wouldn't and decided not to bring it up. It could wait and most probably the situation would work itself out.

As Smith went over the documents for the State Education Commission, Jones was impressed by the progress the campus had made in the past two years. The role and mission statement, agreed upon by the faculty senate as well as the Board of Regents, reflected Linden State's transition from a state teachers college to a comprehensive university. The doctoral programs in education would be supplemented by doctorates in the arts and sciences and in other professional programs. Emphasis would be placed on developing Linden State's business program, already a center of excellence recognized throughout the region. The importance of publication was recognized in the faculty reward structure, and bold new initiatives were envisioned in public service.

The going had been tough, but the endless planning sessions and committee meetings had paid off. A new institutional consensus had been built. Jones was especially proud of the willingness of the faculty to address the establishment of priorities. It was a difficult time for Linden State's older faculty who were committed to teaching and suspicious of research, but Jones was confident that they would be treated with dignity and their contributions would continue to be respected.

Among the specific programs for which Linden State sought approval from the State Education Commission was a doctor of arts degree in the humanities. Jones had encouraged the development of the proposal. He was anxious that Linden State view itself as a true university and not a "trade school" that put all its eggs in the basket of professional and applied programs. He would have preferred a Ph.D. program but knew that the old-line state university would successfully oppose Linden State's involvement in Ph.D. programs in the arts and sciences. In fact, it was the president of the state university who had suggested the doctor of arts alternative and pledged his institution's assistance and support if it were needed before the Education Commission. The degree would be teaching-oriented and would serve, especially, community college instructors who wished to upgrade their qualifications. It would draw upon the particular strengths of Linden State as a university.

The faculty and dean of the arts and sciences wanted to hold out for a Ph.D. program but eventually they went along with the D.A. notion. They had rolled up their sleeves and developed what Jones believed to be an innovative and academically sound program proposal.

The new general education package developed by the faculty would be the major focus of Jones' presentation to the Education Commission. An academic conservative, he liked the program's new, or old, direction. The revolution of the 1960s was in disarray; the counterrevolution was gaining ground. He remembered how a faculty member had described the change in general education. "We have replaced the old cafeteria approach with a menu from a good restaurant. By ordering from this menu, each student will be assured of a nutritious, balanced meal that will further the healthy development of his mind." Jones liked the analogy better the first time he had heard it. He wouldn't use it at the Commission meeting.

Chairman Schultz of the Board of Regents would make the trip with Jones and Smith to the capital for the meeting. Schultz could speak about the board's enthusiasm for the Linden State academic master plan, and he was especially supportive of the general education reform. Like many successful businessmen, he supported a toughening up of the curriculum.

The State Education Commission was located on the sixth floor of the State Office Building, about a block and a half down from the capitol. The commission had been established in the 1950s by the legislature to bring about needed planning and coordination in higher education. However, it was the accepted wisdom that the state's governance system for higher education was still chaotic and should be reformed. It was also the accepted wisdom that no one could come upon a politically acceptable solution. The various educational institutions all thought that the commission was always seeking to expand its role and to evolve into a "super board." The legislature, which established the commission, was viewed as the principal force behind the move, but there were still many legislators whose loyalties were to the various institutions and so there was a stalemate of sorts. Each year, however, there was a new statute adding some power to the commission. There was even talk of giving the commission substantial power over higher education budgets, and Jones wondered what it would be like to avoid the yearly debacle of the budget committee hearing.

There were also constant rumors that the legislature was considering the abolition of the commission. A new super board would be established, or the elected regents of the state university would be asked to take over the governance of all the university-level campuses and even the state colleges. Jones was glad that Linden State had its own board, and he certainly did not want his institution to be a stepchild of the state university under the elected regents.

As they went up the elevator, Jones found himself wondering about the wisdom of locating the offices of a higher education commission or board so near the capitol. The proximity to the seat of political power and intrigue seemed to foster a political atmosphere among the commission staff. They always seemed to have the inside dope, a finger on the pulse of the legislature, and a superior attitude toward presidents like Jones from the outlying areas.

They went first to the main reception area, and Smith set out to inquire about the place of the meeting. Jones took the opportunity to look around and noticed that something was different from his last visit. The internal walls had been removed and the state's latest plan for landscaped offices had been implemented. He shuddered inwardly when he thought about the movement to bring Linden State first under state purchasing, then state personnel, and who knew what else. He could also better appreciate why the commission had not been a champion of improving the faculty office situation at Linden State.

Jones' first experience with landscaped offices had been with Linden State's new library. It was to be built according to an open modular system that provided for great flexibility in the use of space as the library's needs changed. He learned that meant saving the state money by eliminating internal walls, and if the ceilings of the building had been higher he may have had the opportunity to toy with the idea of using the university's most sacred building, its library, for the intramural basketball program. Linden State was developing a program justification for a new administration building to house the student affairs staff. He made a note to tell Bashford that there was no need to hurry the proposal. It was better to allow some time for the landscaped offices craze to pass. He wouldn't bear the responsibility for pushing the student affairs people from their creative environment in Old Main to the kind of sterile and confused environment he now saw before him.

Smith tugged at Jones' suit coat. The meeting was in conference room 660A-B. Regent Schultz was already on his way down the hall and was greeted by the commission's executive director. Jones joined them in time to hear the executive director's apology that the commission could not hold the meeting at Linden State, so students and faculty could attend and so the newer commissioners could see the university first hand. The commission wanted to get a better feel for each institution, so it could do a better job of understanding and supporting them. He hoped that Linden State would invite them down some time soon.

The presentation went well. Chairman Schultz expressed the great pride the board had in Linden State and drew some spontaneous laughter when—tongue in cheek—he said the board looked forward to its role in the 1980s. Jones was well prepared, and Smith did a superb job of handling questions from the committee staff, who had reviewed the academic master plan. Interruptions from the commission members themselves were few in number and they appeared to pay close attention.

Toward the close of the meeting, Chairman Olson of the commission praised Jones and Linden State for the creative and sound way they had gone about responding to the commission's new format for academic master plans. He wished some of the other institutions had done as well and seemed to sneer at the state university liaison representative at the back of the conference room. Olson, though, did have one major policy issue that he would like to discuss with Jones.

"I like your efforts in general education, especially the new interdisciplinary courses that you're developing. But I do have a related concern. Your curriculum is going to end up being unique in the state, and my concern is about the ability of community college students to transfer to your institution and to do well. You've done a good job of responding to this commission's and this state's concern for improving academic quality. However, we must also be concerned about student access to our universities, especially the access enjoyed by students who must attend community colleges because they cannot afford to move away from home for four full years or because they're shy on the grade points needed to get into our universities right after high school."

"The commission has talked about this problem off and on for some time," Olson went on, "and your presentation today highlights why it is important that we go ahead with the statewide study of general education requirements and community college transfer opportunities that we've had in mind. I would like to indicate that I am going to appoint a task force to look into the whole area and make recommendations to us. I believe that this is also an area where the legislature has some interests. In addition, I'll be asking the individual campus governing boards to give us some names of potential task force members."

The executive director and the commission staff members couldn't completely hide their pleasure with how things were going. Nor could the institutional attendees hide their apprehension.

"I have a little different concern with the Linden State master plan." The particular commission member who made that remark had been silent throughout the earlier discussions. "I just can't see Linden State getting into arts and sciences doctorates. That's not Linden State's role. We don't need more doctorates in the arts and sciences, and I think we have here another example of a university aggrandizing itself for its internal reasons without considering the needs of the state and its limited resources. I know there's some debate about this commission's purview in academic planning, but it is clear that we have the direct statutory responsibility to approve, or not to approve, new degree programs. The legislature gave us that responsibility because the institutional governing boards were too close to the campuses and would approve everything. I'm going to vote against the D.A., or whatever it is, program at Linden State, and as far as I am concerned the state university is the only place that ought to be giving out doctorates in the arts and sciences."

In the debate that followed Jones did his best, but he knew early on that he was going to lose. Maybe he would have gotten one or two more votes if there had not been the awkward exchange about the support he had received from the state university for the doctor of arts proposal. He thought that a few commissioners saw the skilled hand of the state university behind the whole effort and thus grew more determined to assert the commission's authority then and there.

The vote to turn down the doctorate was seven to two. The rest of the academic master plan was approved by a vote of nine to zero, with a proviso that the general education portion was subject to further review once the commission's task force made its report. The commission also took the time to endorse perfunctorily the chairman's proposal for the task force, adding the provision that there should be full voting members from the institutional governing boards. A discussion about equal representation for universities, the state colleges, and the community colleges was cut short due to a lack of time, but Olson summarily said he would take into account the various views that had been brought out when he made the appointments.

Jones drove on the way back to Linden State. He and Schultz had what they thought was a most interesting discussion about the direction that higher education governance was likely to take. Smith was quiet. General education revisions were most painful for a university, and he dreaded the possibility of the commission's task force reopening the whole issue. He also dreaded meeting with the arts and sciences dean to tell him about the demise of the doctor of arts proposal.

That night Jones composed a letter to Chairman Olson of the State Education Commission. An essential point had not been brought out in the discussion of the membership of the task force on general education and student access. It was most important that the faculty be represented on the task force. Still better, he wrote, each institution should be asked for its thoughts about the concerns Olson had expressed. That would allow for full faculty participation in the development of such important educational policies, and the commission would benefit from the insights of the various university and college faculties.

The value of the commission's efforts could be seen, Jones granted generously, in its cogent criticisms of Linden State's doctor of arts proposal. He had found the discussion fair and enlightening. However, the commission suffered from inadequacies not of its own making and at times skated on thin ice through which the campus as well as the commission could fall into treacherously cold water. (He would come back and edit that, Jones thought.) The commission was distant from the campuses and did not have an opportunity to appreciate the manner in which a truly good university functions. In particular, it lacked close exposure to a university faculty.

The faculty was central to the university. They were not employees of the university; they were its officers. They alone had the expertise to develop the university's curriculum. They properly controlled the university's instructional programs. Olson would not want a social scientist like Jones controlling and determining the science, humanities, and professional school curricula, would he? (Why wasn't it "curriculi"? Jones wondered.)

Likewise, the faculty in essence controlled the university's research program. No university president could simply order his faculty to be creative. Instead the task of a president was to ensure that the university facilitated the creative endeavors of his faculty.

Public service programs were successful due to the energies of the faculty and their willingness to share their expertise in an applied manner with the world around them.

The university was a professional organization. As members of a profession, faculty members were all peers and thus approached their work through committees, through the development of consensus and, where necessary, by voting. The issues were complicated and weighty; the process demanding and arduous. But outcomes far superior to those that would come forth from administrators justified the efforts.

Jones then came more to the point. Did Chairman Olson have any idea of the havoc that would be caused by a commission action that would overturn two years of work by the faculty of Linden State in developing its general education revisions? The results would be so abhorrent to the integrity of Linden State that all of Jones' efforts in academic planning, so praised by the commission, would be for naught. The commission should cease and desist from further consideration of general education before disaster struck.

Jones read over what he had written up to this point. He wouldn't send it. His points were good but the tone was wrong. He would work on it later. For some reason he drew at the end of the uncompleted letter an upside down triangle. For some reason he couldn't put his finger on, his mood was somber.

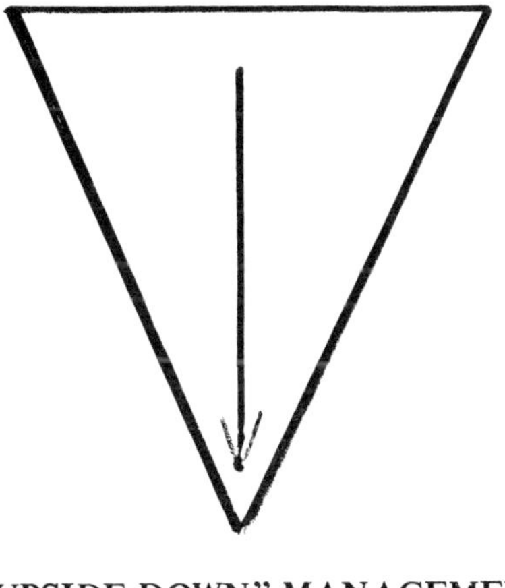

"UPSIDE-DOWN" MANAGEMENT

A good university was organized as a professional organization. The faculty of the university controlled the university's ends—teaching, research, and public service. They were the true bosses. The administration of the university was responsible for providing the means that enabled the faculty to do its work in as supportive an environment as possible. That was the ideal to which Jones had been committed since he had first become a faculty member.

When he revised the letter, however, he would add a paragraph about the role and responsibilities of the president as the university's chief academic officer and as the leader of his faculty. His mind also flashed back to the memoranda he had read that morning about the instructional equipment audit and the School of Social Science. If the faculty truly ran the university, wouldn't it be a glorious and exciting place, but in the long run one without enough funds to accomplish its purposes. In turn, if administrators were too much in charge, all the rules might be followed but wouldn't the university be a deadly place lacking the vitality and experimentation so necessary for it to be true to its nature. Wasn't there need for a balance, for a blend, between the influence of the faculty and the administrators? Ends and means aren't so easily separated.

Jones tucked the letter into the same drawer that contained his earlier ruminations on "top-down" and "bottoms-up" management.

Chapter Four

Jones knew it would be a very full day. He had told Jean to set up meetings with the campus attorney, Smith and Farber, and Bashford and Ken Kauffman, then lunch with Chairman Schultz, and finally a session with the faculty executive committee in his office. Smith and Farber had some sort of scheduling conflict, so he would see Farber in the morning and Smith in the afternoon. Just as well, he thought to himself.

Jean warned him that he was taking on too much in one day. He could do it, he felt, although he was mindful of the fact that he was unable to sustain the energy levels of his earlier years. Wasn't he too young to be growing older?

Jones wanted to tie up loose ends before he went overseas for nine days to visit the foreign campuses that hosted Linden State students. Schultz had enouraged him to take the trip. It would be good for him. And the timing was good, too. Last night when the Joneses hosted the student government leaders for a barbeque at the president's residence, he had been tired. Sure, he enjoyed himself; he always did when he was around the students, especially in the spring when they could see their way through to the end of the year and became more lighthearted.

Linden State provided the Joneses with a magnificent house, off campus, that had been donated by one of the town's leading citizens. It made entertaining easy and the Joneses made full use of it. Jones himself marveled at the way his wife adjusted to the demands placed on a president's wife. He had also remembered her comment, "You should thank food service again,

Hubert. They do such a terrific job for us on these things." Food service needs all the praise they can get, he thought as he put in the call.

The meeting with the campus attorney had some real urgency to it. The attorney wanted to recommend an out-of-court settlement with a faculty member who had been terminated by Peabody and Smith. There were some procedural irregularities, especially by the University Board, and the proposed settlement was small enough that it would be more than covered by the cost savings of not having to go to court. The faculty member was employed elsewhere and seemed to want a symbolic victory more than a financial one. Jones and the attorney went over the case in some detail and then agreed. The campus attorney would firm up an agreement with the faculty member's attorney and then recommend the settlement to Chairman Schultz.

Next they discussed the three other cases in litigation concerning employees, the two suits brought by former employees, the one brought by the staff employees' union, and the three brought by students.

The attorney apologized before bringing up the other items—he knew Jones was pressed for time, but each matter had some urgency to it. So he went over the status of the two investigations by the regional Department of Education office and the one by the state Fair Employment Practices Commission. Then he wanted Jones' reaction to two of the staff grievances and a faculty grievance that were in progress.

The meeting had run fifteen minutes longer than was planned, and Jones was glad when it ended. His attitude toward litigation was similar to Smith's. He wished somehow the university could govern itself, that people would be satisfied with the various internal review processes that had been set up, but he knew it was too much to hope for.

Dean Farber didn't look irritated that he had had to wait.

"Sorry that Smith and I couldn't get our schedules straightened out," he started. "That was a fun get-together last night. A great success. The students always appreciate the invitation to the president's house."

Jones thought to himself that it truly was a fun evening. He was glad that many of the students had brought their bathing suits, and he enjoyed watching their clowning on the diving board. The highlight of the evening was when Mabel Farber fully dressed, fell in the pool. She took it wonderfully, announcing that she knew there was a reason why she had brought her bathing suit. Both Farbers then put on their suits and joined the fun, staying at the shallow end, Jones noticed. He wished he had felt free enough to join them, but he didn't. Besides he was very conscious of his bulging mid-section. He had to cut down on those big lunches and shouldn't touch those banquet desserts, his wife kept reminding him.

"Mabel laughed all the way home. Good thing, though, that there were only soft drinks and punch around. Wouldn't want any rumors about that the Farbers were on the bottle. Say, you sure were involved in an awfully serious discussion with our student body president and vice president. They're good lobbyists, aren't they."

Jones went over the student body leaders' agenda. They wanted students to serve on the faculty's personnel committees. They were angry because they thought some faculty wanted to sabotage the new student evaluation process and were watching closely the faculty senate's consideration of a proposal that each student be required to sign his evaluation form. They also wanted student majorities on the food service committee and the Board for Auxiliaries. Finally, they were enthusiastic about their plan to hire a lobbyist to look out for student interests and to support Linden State in the legislature.

Jones went over his responses. He would not support the students in their effort to serve on faculty personnel committees. Yes, he was sympathetic to student participation and recognized that student evaluations were important in promoting good teaching. He was not pushing a "publish or perish" attitude at Linden State. He would talk to the faculty executive committee about the student signature issue and had some ideas as to how it could be worked out to satisfy the major concerns of the students and the faculty. He didn't think the idea of a student majority on the Board for Auxiliaries was feasible, but perhaps the number of student representatives could be increased. He would discuss the matter with Dean Farber. He stopped short of discussing food service when his wife and some other students joined them, and he purposely avoided the student lobbyist proposal. He wasn't as enthusiastic about the notion as the student officers were. All in all, he was pleased and surprised by the polite reaction to his comments. Things had changed a great deal since the 1960s.

"Yes," Farber noted, "the students today are much easier to work with than those of the sixties. Back then I used to debate for hours with idealistic students who wished to reform our society, starting with the university, and to make it truly democratic. Students are the consumers of education and they should have an equal voice with the faculty. Better yet, they argued, the faculty senate should become a university senate that reflected the principle of 'one man, one vote.' Or 'one person, one vote,' I should say. You weren't at Linden State then. We were lucky. A few demonstrations and a lot of debate. No violence."

"The students today have some of the same goals as the students of the past, but they're much more willing to compromise. In student affairs we try to work as closely with them as possible. We have our ups and downs and disagreements, but things seem to go along all right. I hope you agree with that?"

Jones indeed agreed and was thankful to have Farber as the dean of student affairs.

Farber went over his own reactions to the topics that Jones and the students discussed. Jones had come down on the faculty-student issues about where Farber thought he would. He had earlier given his opinion on Jones' views to the student officers. It wasn't reasonable to give the students a majority on the Board of Auxiliaries, which served as the governing board for the student union, the book store, the cafeterias, and the dormitories. Among other things, the bond covenants wouldn't permit it. Farber was sympathetic toward increasing student representation on the board, but it was chaired by Bashford and he didn't think that Bashford would agree with him. Bashford and he would discuss it some more. The food service committee was under the Board of Auxiliaries, and Bashford and Farber had already agreed to a student majority on the committee. The director of food services wouldn't be happy about it, which disturbed Bashford.

They would emphasize, however, that any actions of the food service committee were recommendations to the director or to the Board of Auxiliaries, where the administration had a clear majority and Bashford was the chairman.

The complexity of Linden State's auxiliaries still baffled Jones and he was doubly grateful for Farber and Bashford.

"Do you have anything else we should go over before my trip?" Jones asked while sneaking a peek at his watch.

"Nothing that's pressing," Farber replied. "I might mention that Smith and I have asked the faculty executive committee to add the counselors to the faculty senate. The counselors aren't happy with the way the staff council is going. They'd like to be added to the faculty senate like the librarians were."

"What kind of reaction did you get?" Jones asked, trusting that the answer would be brief.

"As you might expect, not a positive one. The faculty is mad at us to start with because they think student affairs is supporting the students in their push to get on the faculty personnel committees. Somehow the discussion even got around to taking the librarians back out of the senate, but Smith managed to kill it off quickly. Well, you have a great deal to do if you're going to get on that plane tomorrow and not carry all baggage around here with you. Let me get out of your hair."

Next came the meeting with Bashford and Ken. They went over the final touches on their response to the audit on instructional equipment. Jones trusted their judgment and hoped that the response would be all right.

Ken brought Jones up to date on the budget. His contact on the budget committee staff had called that morning. The budget committee had met into the early hours of the morning and had reached some agreements that the staff member thought would hold. Lindon State would receive some money to support organized research for the first time and the funds to complete the renovation of the computer center. The rest of the news wasn't as good. There would be added funds for 300 more students, even though the university was already some 800 students over budget. The committee was skeptical that enrollments would hold up in the 1980s; they were already hearing from the public schools that their enrollments were going down. The student-faculty ratio would go up some, so Linden State would not get all the positions they might expect. Moreover, the committee had written in a footnote that the new positions should go to the business and architecture programs. A footnote wasn't binding, but it could be ignored only at an institution's peril.

Haynes had wanted to give Linden State a higher student enrollment number and no new faculty. Foster and Barnes came to the rescue. In fact, the committee staff member indicated that Barnes and Haynes really got into it but then caught himself and never gave any details.

The rest of the budget was what Linden State could expect. Although the state talked a good game of "program budgeting" and "management by objectives," the numbers were derived by the usual formulas.

Oh, yes, there was one other matter. The budget committee was considering appropriating all funds for instructional equipment to the State Education Commission. The commission would then establish criteria, receive requests, and allocate the funds to the individual campuses.

Bashford, Ken, and Jones went through a ritualistic bemoaning of the folly of the budget committee. Jones added that Ken had better get to Smith right away. For recruitment purposes, Smith had made some tentative allocations of faculty positions that were based on a significantly higher number than Linden State was now going to get.

"Say, Bob, I was curious about one other thing. How's the new staff council going?" Jones asked.

"Not very well, to be frank," Bashford replied. The staff council didn't like the fact that it made its recommendations to Bashford instead of the president. They wanted a structure that paralleled that established for the faculty. The supervisors were irritated in many cases because they thought they were being undermined. The discussion on the parking and traffic plan had blown up. It was early in the game, however, and Bashford thought it would start to go better.

Jones had made up fifteen minutes. He had some time to sign papers and return a few phone calls.

As he dutifully signed the many papers Jean handed him, he heard her say, "This does it, Dr. Jones. Everything else can wait until you get back." They had learned that Jones didn't need to concentrate while he was scribbling his name and could carry on a conversation or at least follow what Jean was saying. "Be sure to get in some sightseeing. It's too bad, though, that you couldn't have gone earlier. Spring in Linden is my favorite time of the year. While you're gone, I'll open up the windows and get some fresh air in here."

Jones didn't like the remark about the windows, and he suspected that Jean and his wife had been discussing his smoking habit again. Some day he'd put down the pipe forever, but not now.

"Why don't I move your meeting with the executive committee to another time. You could meet with them when you get back from Europe. They would understand."

"No. I want to get it over with before my trip."

Jones was running late for his luncheon. Henry Schultz was a good guy, but he was still the chairman of the Board of Regents and Jones hoped he wasn't there already. Jones had been caught in traffic and the parking spaces right by the restaurant had been taken. He spotted a tight spot down the street that he might take. At times like these he was glad the university motor pool had only small economy cars and thanked Senator Foster. He tried twice to back into the cramped space, felt embarrassed by the beeping horns on the busy street, and allowed himself the luxury of the expensive parking lot down from the restaurant. As he turned the keys over to the attendant, he mentally justified the expenditure to an auditor on the grounds that he shouldn't keep the chairman of the board waiting.

Schultz had been seated for only a few minutes and had ordered each of them a glass of chablis. Jones glanced at the menu and decided quickly on the catch of the day. In his own mind he couldn't decide if he ordered fish because his mother had told him it was brain food or because he thought his wife had told him it was low in calories. Of course the sauce wouldn't help.

"I appreciate your being able to join me for lunch," Jones started out. "Sorry I'm late."

"I don't mind at all, Hubert. That's one of the joys of being semi-retired. You have some time. Now relax a bit. Jean told me this morning that you don't have to get back until two o'clock."

Jones couldn't relax. He hated to discuss business while eating and had developed the habit of getting everything of consequence over, whenever he could, before his food was served.

First he brought Schultz up to date on the status of the budget. Schultz wasn't surprised by any of the information and added that Barnes earlier in the week had stopped him at the symphony concert intermission and had underscored the need for the campus to develop its business program. In turn, Schultz had put in a word for some funding for research. Linden State was counting on Barnes to help it become a full-fledged university.

Schultz added that the mayor had talked to him about widening Ash Street on the western perimeter of the campus to accommodate four lanes of traffic. He had told the mayor that the board would look at the proposal, but he didn't expect it to respond with much enthusiasm. Would Jones have Bashford and the planning people prepare a background piece for the next board meeting?

Schultz sensed that the food was about to be served and was aware of Jones' idiosyncracy about heavy discussions while he was eating, so he would have to hurry the one other serious matter on his own agenda.

"I want you to know that the board at its last executive session voted to extend your contract by three years. We can talk about the details later, but I thought it might be nice for you to know ahead of your trip.

"We're very pleased with how things are going at the university. The community feels good about the campus. Of course the fact that the football team took the conference championship and that the basketball team had a winning season helped. But more important than that, as a board we are very pleased with the way Linden State, despite its problems, is coming along as a university."

"Anything special I should be concerned about, Henry?"

"No, I don't think so. As you might guess, the board is going to have to be tougher about its role in academic matters. We can't have another go around like that doctor of arts fiasco. We'll talk some more when you get back, and the board's personnel committee will want to hold a formal evaluation meeting with you. When we hired you we knew we were jumping you ahead pretty far and fast, but we're pleased with the way you're learning. Let's put the topic aside for now. Here comes your food."

Jones enjoyed his meal, and if he had not been going to a meeting he would have had another glass of wine with Henry.

After dessert, Schultz quipped, "It's getting close to two o'clock. It's bad enough being late for lunch with the chairman of the board, but you don't want to get yourself in real trouble by standing up the faculty executive committee. I've been around the university long enough to know that."

They left the restaurant together and Schultz asked casually about Albert Smith. He hadn't seen much of him lately. Jones thanked Schultz and the board for their show of confidence in him and was glad he was parked so close to the restaurant. He wouldn't be late for the meeting with the faculty.

On the way back to the campus Jones thought some more about Schultz's inquiry concerning his vice president for academic affairs and wondered why he had not responded. Smith had been having a rough time, especially with the faculty senate on the promotions procedure. Well, he thought to himself, nearly everything had been worked out. The few differences that were left were important in terms of asserting that the vice president was expected to exercise independent judgment. On that point Smith was right not to compromise, and Jones would stand by him.

The meeting with the faculty executive committee went better than Jones had expected, partly because Smith wasn't there. The executive committee would recommend that the senate accept the administration's version of the last points in contention. The discussion was drawn out and often obscure, but that was the bottom line. They respected Smith, even though they disagreed with him, and for the past two years he had not, in their words, repeated his "arbitrary and distasteful actions." The executive committee thought that the senate as a whole would go along. There would be some loud noises from the faculty union types, but what they wanted was collective bargaining, not "faculty governance."

The chairman of the executive committee also reported on his testimony before the Assembly Committee on State Personnel. The committee was considering a bill to authorize collective bargaining for state employees. As the executive committee had discussed, its chairman focused on the need for any such bill to take into account the peculiarities of the state's universities. Provision would have to be made for the continuance of faculty senates, along side any bargaining agent. In response to a question, he had indicated that he personally did not favor collective bargaining, but that he thought the faculty should be covered by such a bill. The faculty as a whole should have the opportunity to vote on the issue of collective bargaining and make its choice. The hearing also gave him a good chance to tell the legislators that unless the faculty received higher salaries and other support he would guess that the unions would gain ground.

Three other faculty from Linden State had spoken in favor of collective bargaining. The chairman of the executive committee was pleased with the hearing as a whole and recommended that the issue be considered further at the committee's next meeting. Jones sensed at this point that the committee wished that he, as well as Smith, wasn't there. He considered bringing up the student signature issue, but decided to leave well enough alone for one day. The meeting ended on a very cordial note.

Jones was running late again. It was already 3:15 and his appointment with Smith was supposed to be at 3:00. It wasn't until twenty minutes later that Smith came in. It wasn't like him.

"Sorry I'm late," Smith said. "I know there are many items we should go over before your trip, but if you don't mind I need to talk about something else.

"As you know, I've had a hard time lately. The battle with the senate over the promotions process hasn't been any fun and has gotten me down. The social science faculty is after me, and there are still some scars left over from the general education debate. Ken told me about the budget figures, and I am not looking forward to another round with either the business school or the arts and sciences. I hardly had the stomach to meet with the humanities faculty about the doctor of arts the other day, and I wanted to hit that son-of-a-bitch dean in the mouth. I can't believe that they have forgotten that for fourteen years I was a teaching member of the English department and that I served as chairman of the department for six years before I became the dean of the faculty. Of couse, I can't blame them if they forget; sometimes I hardly remember myself.

"I'm also so damn tired of the grievances. Six years ago, when I became vice president for academic affairs, I thought I would put all the personnel crap behind me. Unfortunately I never could find a new dean of the faculty who could satisfy me. I guess I just carried on with what I thought I could do better than anyone else, but the faculty has changed through the years, more than I have. So many things we used to handle informally are now subject to elaborate procedures. And it seems that anytime anyone is really dissatisfied, the first thing they do is file a grievance. At first I tried to iron things out to everyone's mutual benefit, but now I'm afraid I just try to beat the bastards.

"I want you to know that I've tried my best to work things out with the senate on the promotions procedure, but I don't think I've made it. Realistically, I have become a liability to you. I think you know that."

"That's not true," Jones interjected. "I met with the executive committee today and think we have things worked out. They have a lot of respect for you, regardless of any disagreement they and you might have had."

"Thanks, Hubert, but it goes much deeper than that. I understand where the university is going and, in the abstract, don't disagree with the emphasis on professional programs. But, it is not going any place that is satisfying to me as a person and to my own values. It's going some place that I don't want to go. I came here believing in the liberal arts, and my happiest years were when we were making the old education faculty turn tail and run. Now it's our turn to run and I don't like it. I especially don't like being the henchman who brings it about. Maybe that's why I hate being the middleman between the programs that are swallowing everything up, like business, and the arts and sciences. My time has come, Hubert. What I'm obviously telling you is that I'm resigning as vice president for academic affairs.

"Is it anything I've done?" Jones asked. "Is there something that I can do to help? I don't want you to resign."

"No, it's not anything you've done. I appreciate the changes and the more open attitude you've brought to the campus. The faculty now accepts some things that Peabody tried to force upon them, and that's good. No, it goes beyond anything you've done. Maybe it goes back to when Mary died, nine years ago. Since that time Linden State has become my life and I've not had much else. I know that it's time for me and for Linden State that I move on. I only hope that it's not too late for either of us."

"What do you plan to do? Go back to teaching?"

"I'm not sure. I think I'd like to, but I'm not sure whether I want to return to the department. I think maybe I could afford to retire. Between my pension and some royalties I still get I'd probably do all right."

"You know that the board would approve a sabbatical for you."

"That might be the way to go. My doctor has been urging me to take some time off. I guess the pressure's starting to get to me."

"Why don't you think it all over," Jones said. "Let's talk about it when I get back from my trip. I would hope that you might feel differently about things then."

"I don't think so but all right. Sorry to lay this on you just before the trip. I didn't want to . . . but I had to."

"They didn't talk anymore. Smith left and Jones was alone. Jean had been right. He had taken on too much in one day.

He had gone from an emotional high at lunch, when he learned that his own contract had been extended, to a new low now with Smith, and had been at all levels in between. There was too much pain for him to handle in the tone of Smith's voice and in what he had to say. Jones was sorry, but he couldn't help his friend Albert, at least not now.

(Three days later, while Jones was away, Smith sent his formal resignation letter. He told no one else until Jones had had the opportunity to discuss the resignation with the board and had sent out the formal announcement to the faculty.)

Jones stayed up late that night. All the bags had been packed for his trip. He had placed his passport and tickets in the pocket of the suit coat he would wear the next day. His wife had urged him to come to bed, but she understood his need to be by himself. He shrugged off her concerns about his getting his rest with a comment that he had practiced and had fully developed the fine art of sleeping on an airplane. He was glad that she had come in to kiss him good night and had not felt the need to say anything more.

For a while he simply listened to some records that he had put on the stereo, a curious mixture of classical and gospel music. For some reason he couldn't understand, they reflected his mood, or perhaps, he hoped, they might raise his spirits.

Somehow he had to make sense out of the day. He was surprised and dismayed by Smith's desire to resign. But was he really so surprised? Why had he ignored Schultz's inquiry? Had they both known? He felt no malice that Smith had destroyed the best laid plans he and Jean had made to ensure that he would go off on his European trip feeling caught up and at ease. Smith would resign, he thought, and he didn't blame him. Smith owed no one, and especially him, anything more.

He had pressed too much into one day, had seen too much of the university in too short a time. The whole thing was chaotic. It was adversarial. So many of the university's members cried out that they were aggrieved. He was not a practitioner of "top-down," "bottoms-up," or "upside-down" management. Perhaps "top-versus-bottom" best described the university. Perhaps the university would be best off in a collective bargaining arrangement. At least collective bargaining accepted the legitimacy and pervasiveness of conflict and provided a mechanism for resolving differences. He had always been opposed to collective bargaining, especially for the faculty, but now he wasn't so sure. If it eventually did come, he determined he would try to make the most of it, but it still didn't seem to him to be the answer.

It had been a difficult year: the budget committee hearing, the campus energy savings fiasco, the Education Commission's review of Linden State's master plan. But wasn't that the nature of the university. Weren't there always such goings-on. He was down because of Smith's resignation and understandably so.

Jones went over to his desk and pulled out the notes he had made after the various crises of the year. That was it. Each triangle represented only one aspect of the university. He would put them together and add a circle around them for good measure to represent the "democratic" or "client-oriented" conceptions of the university that he and Farber had discussed today, a university without a hierarchy or formal structure through which directions were channeled.

"UP-TIGHT" MANAGEMENT

As Jones circled the resulting star he felt better. It was beginning to make sense to him. He was privileged to preside over that wonderful chaos called Linden State University. True, his job so often was daily exercise in "up-tight" management. He was on top of very little, but he was not on the bottom. His world spun in crazy ways. His task was somehow to move the university forward, both to minimize the conflicts that had the potential to fracture the university and to make use of other conflicts so that the university could continue its development.

To be honest, he liked his work and was very pleased when Henry had told him the board had extended his contract by three years. It was not yet his time and, remembering Smith, he prayed that he would know when his time had come. He would go on that European trip, come back to finish up the semester, thoroughly enjoy himself at commencement, and then start another year. He felt better now and would go to bed. He hoped his wife would still be awake. He wanted to talk and wished she could go with him to Europe.

Chapter Five

President Jones liked commencement day more than any other. It was a day of joy and recognition. The university in its magnificent wholeness gathered to honor and then send on their way its charges. He had worked hard on his remarks this year, but they had come out the same as those he had made the year before. "The day marked a passage from one stage of life to another." Maybe that's why he enjoyed it. For him it marked the end of one academic year and the promise of another.

He thought his bright orange Princeton doctoral robe added to the dignity of the event. He always wanted one and could now both afford it and justify it. He had read somewhere that the president's robe was supposed to be distinctive.

He admitted to Jean and his wife that the orange robe made their task of selecting new robes for the Board of Regents more difficult. He left the decision of whether to order green or yellow ones, the university colors, to Jean and his wife but he would wear orange. They had decided upon a green color that went rather well.

The students were in a good mood as always. One of Jones' reforms was to move commencement to the morning from the evening in order to maximize the proportion of sober students. At the evening commencement the year before, he had been afraid to slow down for fear that things would get out of control. Inwardly Jones shared the students' euphoria.

As he stood before the assembled throng in the football stadium, Jones was amazed by the turnout from the faculty. Perhaps the debate stirred up by the acting dean of social sciences had had the desired effect. He shouldn't be so quick to judge the consequences of others' efforts.

The whole event went remarkably well. He felt great pride in the special recognition for the student body president, who had won a Woodrow Wilson Fellowship and would attend Michigan, and especially for the class valedictorian, who had won a Princeton National Fellowship. There were loud cheers and popping champagne corks when he mentioned the football team's conference championship, and the whole scene was surprisingly repeated when he cited the accomplishments of the football guard who had made an academic all-American team.

Smith handled his duties as vice president for academic affairs with remarkable calm, and the highlight of the day for Jones came near the close of the ceremony when the chairman of the board read a plaque citing Smith's accomplishments. The first to stand in Smith's honor was the dean of arts and sciences, followed by the entire English department, and then the remaining faculty who were present. They had come *en masse* to honor their own, and Jones felt that Smith now knew that he had not stayed on too long as far as Linden State was concerned.

The students joined in the observance for Smith. The rest of the champagne corks flew as did all the paper airplanes fashioned from commencement programs during the president's address. By the time the families and friends joined in, a first class melee was underway. The stadium had not witnessed so much sound and fury since Linden State's last touchdown in November. When the mortar boards started to fly every which way, Jones couldn't help but notice a small smile across Smith's face.

There was a brief moment of calm that Jones seized to ask the audience to join in the singing of Linden State's alma mater, which he dedicated on this particular occasion to Smith. The latter action wasn't in the program, but Jones thought that Smith might like it.

Jones was glad he was at the front of the recessional line after the alma mater. He hurried along, noticeably so, which bothered him because he didn't want people to see that tears were forming in his eyes. Jones believed that presidents were not supposed to cry.

It had been a difficult year. He would take a few days off and then complete his reorganization plan. If he was going to get any real vacation he would have to act quickly. There was the request budget to finish up and the preparations for the Budget Committee hearing in the early fall.

The Joneses had been away for nearly a week when the final pieces of the reorganization plan became clear. He closeted himself and made enough notes so that he could put the issue aside for the weekend. On Monday he would write out the details of the plan. By then the students and faculty would be gone for the summer; he would have a chance to think and write. He should start preparing the new budget book. Mustn't get on that now, he thought to himself.

Jones had struggled with a way in which to minimize the inherent stress in the university between administrative, or hierarchical, authority and the professional authority that lay with the faculty. He recognized that administrative amateurs from the faculty, such as he, were named presidents of universities because they understood and respected the ways of the faculty. As a social scientist, however, he wasn't satisfied with the manner in which his colleagues dismissed administration as an arbitrary, power-oriented endeavor in necessary conflict with the rational activities of the faculty. He also smarted from the faculty's dismissal of academic administrators as basically good fellows, at least when they started their terms, but always second rate. Perhaps he smarted because he feared that in his case there might be truth in the observation.

Hadn't Max Weber characterized "bureaucratic authority" as "rational authority"? Jones would develop an administrative organization that would encourage rational decision making. He would place directly under him one person responsible for academic affairs, another for business affairs, and a third for student affairs. That way, when they met as a group, all of the fundamental concerns of the university and its constituencies would be represented. Something was missing. As president of the university, he would take on the added responsibility of explicitly relating the university to its external environment. Jones also knew that he personally would be more comfortable knowing that he was regularly exposed to a diverse management group that represented the various concerns and constituencies of the university. He was less likely to be blind-sided.

He sensed another advantage in the organizational pattern he had outlined. It addressed the problem of melding together the various conceptions of the university held by the faculty, staff, and students and communicating effectively with each group. The vice president for academic affairs would be faculty-oriented and predisposed toward "upside down" management. The vice president for business affairs (or should it be for administration, he wondered) would be responsible for relations with the staff; he would exercise a "bottoms up" (and on occasion a "top down") management style. Bashford could handle that. He was working out well with the new staff council despite the original problems. Farber as dean of student affairs would work directly with student government and would be sympathetic toward its "democratic" ways.

The two vice presidents and the dean of students would need to understand and on occasion to adopt the various management styles Jones had outlined. They all had to deal with faculty, staff, and students–individually and in groups such as committees, task forces, and senates–as well as with the staffs of their own offices. They all must become masters of ambiguity and practitioners of "up-tight" management. In that manner they would also develop a better understanding of one another's world.

If the plan was to work, Jones thought, he would have to hold regular meetings with his top aides. Through such meetings he would seek to blend the various concerns of the university's constituent parts into a whole. He also hoped that through the meetings each of his aides would better understand the importance of the others' activities and contributions.

In order to minimize conflict and to preserve options for the president where conflict was not resolved, Jones wished to delegate much authority to his top aides. As president, however, he would still retain a role in academic affairs. To him any other choice would mean that he had turned his back on his responsibilities as the institutional head. Then, too, he would not be effective in dealing with the faculty if he appeared too divorced from educational issues. Finally, he needed to be academically involved for himself.

Jones would assert for the president a major role in long-range academic planning. He would bring especially to the planning process a sensitivity to community and state needs that Linden State must meet if it were to be responsive and vital as a university. And supported by the legislature, he noted. Thus he added a director of institutional research and planning to the persons reporting directly to him. He would be a "staff" as opposed to a "line" officer, Jones envisioned. As he sketched out the position, he hoped that he would enjoy the same close relationship with the new vice president for academic affairs that he had enjoyed with Smith and that the new vice president would not view him as interfering with his own area of responsibility. Incongruously he found himself wondering if the new vice president would have a sense of humor. Somehow the thought seemed very important to Jones.

Ken Kauffman as the university's budget officer would also report directly to him. Jones would tie together the planning and budgeting processes to bring major concerns to his level, to keep his fingers on problem areas, and to give him a way to reach down to details that concerned him. Bashford would accept the formal move of Ken to the president's office. Informally it had worked that way anyway. As president, Jones required direct access to Ken in order to respond to the demands of the Budget Committee. Academic affairs also would be pleased by the move. They suspected that Bashford was using his control over the budget office to rip off the academic programs

Jones would assign to Bashford the various community relations offices that now reported directly to the president. It would cut down his involvement in details. The directors could still come to him when they needed to and he could go directly to them. Bashford would not feel threatened, and Bashford was well thought of in the community and would respond well to a new challenge.

There was another staff officer who would report directly to the president, the affirmative action officer. It would be his way of saying to the university that affirmative action was very important in the years ahead. It would also make his cabinet more "rational" in that currently its members were all "majority males." The new vice president might be a woman or a member of a minority, but that would be so much the better in Jones' opinion.

His wife and kids were looking for him, so he quickly folded the small sheets of paper on which he had made his notes and put them in his wallet so he would not forget them on Monday.

On Monday the effort went well. Jones was fresh. He dictated the first section in a little more than an hour. It would be theoretical and would give him an opportunity to show the Board of Regents what he thought he knew. The notes were very helpful and the points came through clearly now that he was well rested.

He went to lunch with the chairman of the faculty executive committee. The rest of the committee had already departed from campus or were unavailable. The chairman cautioned Jones about rushing the proposal. The faculty would be concerned about the new arrangement for budgeting and academic planning. They would want to know the source of funds for the director of institutional research and planning position. The word "research" should be dropped from the title, to which Jones quickly agreed. It was true that the plan was very similar to that which Jones had discussed earlier with the various faculty committees, but the faculty chairman urged him to wait until the fall when fuller consideration could be given to it. No doubt there would be other concerns that would come up.

Jones would hear of no further delays. He had been "talking reorganization" for the two years that he had been president. The staff had a right to know where they stood, and the board was expecting him to act. If he placed the plan on the faculty's agenda in the fall, it would be another whole year before the plan could be implemented. In the fall he would like the faculty to consider the question of academic reorganization, which was more clearly in their purview. He would bring the plan to the board at its June meeting so it could go into effect with the beginning of the new fiscal year.

His conversation with Bashford went better than he had expected. They had developed a comfortable relationship and Bashford felt that the new community relations arrangement could be made to work. He had no difficulty with Ken's move to the president's office. As to the student affairs move, it wasn't his business but Bashford was relieved that Jones did not contemplate giving student affairs to him. He didn't like to deal with the area.

Farber expressed the reservations that Jones had anticipated. Student affairs had sought to build a solid relationship with the academic programs, and the proposed arrangement might contribute to some added distance between them. On the other hand, it would relieve some of the pressure on whoever became vice president for academic affairs, pressure that was constantly there because so many groups wanted to be viewed as "academic" and central to the university. He would present the reorganization as an upgrading of the student affairs function and would hope for the best. Much he felt would depend on the attitude toward student affairs of the new vice president. If he was sympathetic, then links could be built between the offices. If he were not, then maybe student affairs would be better off on its own.

Jones felt that he had consulted enough over the past two years and that afternoon he finished up his reorganization proposal and arranged a luncheon later in the week with Regents Schultz and Davis, who had been designated by the board to go over the proposal with him.

At lunch Regent Davis was very interested in the introductory section of his reorganization proposal, but she concurred, to Jones' disappointment, with Chairman Schultz's suggestion that he take out the social science jargon. They thought the board would view the reorganization as an administrative matter and that it would be endorsed without difficulty.

At the board meeting Regent Schultz placed Jones' report under "informational items" and asked if any board member had a particular concern with it. No one raised an objection and he declared that Jones would implement the new plan as an administrative action. Jones was pleased by the efficient way Schultz had handled the matter and inwardly thanked Schultz for suggesting after the luncheon that he ask the editor of the budget book to go over the proposal. The edited version was much clearer and raised fewer controversial points.

Jones thought he had noticed a faculty member who wanted to speak to the reorganization plan. In any case, Schultz did not call upon anyone. The board was anxious to get onto its consideration of the recent budget that the legislature had approved for Linden State.

After the meeting had concluded, Jones kept himself busy for a while, hoping that the faculty member who had sought recognition from Chairman Schultz would desert his post by the door. Jones didn't feel up to being hassled. He had come back too soon. Tomorrow he would go off on a longer vacation.

The faculty member introduced himself and Jones recognized the name as that of the old history professor whose memoranda he had read. He was surprised when the former acting dean of social sciences joined them and doubly so when the two faculty members seemed to be on the best of terms. He listened as they went over again all the objections that the chairman of the faculty executive committee had raised and then some.

They objected, in particular, to the way the administration had shown its disdain for the faculty by acting on such an important matter in the summer when the faculty wasn't there, and they suspected that Jones intended to use the same tactic in the case of academic reorganization. The history department was unalterably opposed to any tinkering with the School of Social Sciences. They had struggled mightily to separate themselves from the gargantuan School of Arts and Sciences, and they suspected that Jones wanted to put them back there. They're right on that point, Jones thought, but he had never discussed it with anyone. Jones assured them that it was his intention to have full faculty consultation on the reorganization of the schools. He also added "academic reorganization" to his list of contentious issues that would be before the university during the next year.

Jones stopped by his office before leaving campus. When he saw Jean, he could tell that she had something important to tell him.

"Dr. Jones, Albert came by. We've known each other for years and we had a nice chat. I was sort of surprised, though. He had on an old gray sweatsuit and bright yellow Nikes. He said he was playing handball–something called 'cut-throat'–with his old cronies in education and that I should tell you 'they are beating the heck out of me but I love it anyway,' quote and unquote. He said you'd understand."

Jones wasn't sure he fully did, but he smiled at Jean anyway.

That night Jones pulled together some books that he wanted to read while on vacation. In going over his library, he recognized so many volumes that had influenced his reorganization plan. Maybe he should have reread them before coming to his conclusions. Oh, well, he thought, it is all temporary. After him there would be a new president who would again reorganize to fit the needs of Linden State at that time and to fit his own conception of the university.

He wanted to go down to the bookstore to pick up some mysteries but decided first to finish the book he was reading, Alasdair MacIntyre's *After Virtue.* He had enjoyed MacIntyre's account of emotivism and its derivation. He was bothered by the analysis of Weber and wondered to what extent he himself represented the norms of the "bureaucratic character." That evening he was also richly rewarded. MacIntyre's conclusions to some would seem pessimistic, but to him they had a positive and personal meaning. Jones lived in the tradition of a university community. In that tradition his life and vocation had meaning. He would reread MacIntyre and then turn to something lighter.

Afterword

The concept of "up-tight management" differs somewhat from other views of organizations in that it emphasizes the simultaneous, or mixed, presence of conflict-oriented models along with various models that deemphasize conflict (for example, those based on scientific management, human relations, and professionalism). Academic administrators, professors, ministers, and professionals in social service agencies are examples of groups that most often experience added stress because either they, or others with whom they deal, are committed to ideals, deeply held, that assume conflict is illegitimate. Yet conflict abounds in their worlds.

The stress and conflicts between the faculty as professionals and administrators have been treated at length in the literature of sociology and higher education. These strains are very important to the concept of "up-tight management," but so are others. From the vantage point of a president of a public university, similar pressures and conflicts are found in relations with elected and appointed public officials, state agencies, community groups, support staff, students, and even university support groups. Additionally, a president often faces the dilemma that the more he accommodates the faculty, the more difficulty he faces with other constituencies or participants who take part in the governance of the university. From this perspective, Jones' quest under "up-tight management" may be viewed as an effort to maximize the extent to which he can operate in accordance with professionalism while minimizing the strains with other models.

Jones' university is especially stressful because there are disagreements about the university's goals as well as conflicting process or procedural models. Linden State University is in transition from a teachers college, to a liberal arts college and then to a regional university with a broad array of professional programs. Smith's resignation, for example, is due in part to his inability to cope any longer with his differences with the faculty on procedures, but more fundamentally it results from a disagreement with institutional goals and priorities. He had been personally satisfied with the transition of Linden State from an institution that emphasized teacher education to one that emphasized the liberal arts. He was dissatisfied, however, with the subsequent transition to a regional university that emphasized professional and applied programs and the proactive role that he was required to play in the transition.

Jones placed a high priority on building a consensus on institutional purposes and priorities. In doing so, he sought to emphasize general education and the arts and sciences as well as professional and applied programs. Not everyone, however, is satisfied with a new consensus. Some, like Smith, opt out of active involvement in university governance.

In the narrative there are several indications of stress building within Jones. I would have preferred a lighthearted treatment throughout but, alas, for the purposes of the narrative it is Jones' fate to show signs himself of becoming "up-tight." At least at the close I sent him off on a vacation. Also, at the board's evaluation committee meeting we can count on our good friend Schultz telling him that he has made the typical mistake of a new president: he must do a better job of protecting his time or he really will "grow old young." Moreover, he will start making mistakes in his interpersonal relations that will cost him dearly. It is also my hope that he starts playing handball with Smith. The group should turn to "doubles" rather than "cut-throat."

The narrative reflects my own interests as a practitioner whose academic background is public administration, and I recognize that it does not treat adequately the critical strain between the role demands of Jones' position and his own personality needs. The focus is not on Jones per se, but instead on his situation. Basic to the argument of the narrative is the thesis that the situation leads inexorably to "up-tight management."

Nor is the narrative long on advice to presidents on how to cope personally with stress other than an explicit—and implicit—message that a sense of humor is very helpful. I hope that the reader familiar with a university enjoyed a good laugh now and then as our hero Jones plodded along. In a more serious vein, I hope that the readers of this little volume will develop a greater insight into the stresses and strains within a university and that greater mutual understanding will contribute to producing a more satisfying personal environment.

Although the narrative is written from Jones' perspective as a university president, it is important to underscore that the president is not uniquely a participant in "up-tight management." Faculty, staff, students, and others share in the challenges, ambiguities, and tensions of the situation. I would argue that stress is felt keenly by many participants who have deep commitments to a particular normative model that deemphasizes the legitimacy of conflict only to find that actual behavior within the university falls short of their ideals. In this light, I am sure that a poll of the faculty at Jones' university would show that they do not uniformly share my view that Jones is committed to maximizing professionalism as the dominant style within the university. In turn, it is important that Jones as a president develop a better understanding of the various models that are present in the university in order to increase his own effectiveness, especially in the vital area of communicating with various university constituencies.

In the narrative I may appear to pick on counselors, but it has been for a particular purpose. Counselors and librarians are examples of professional groups that are often placed in a special bind at the interface between two separate university personnel systems based on different organizational models. By education and background they are similar to the teaching faculty and may be included as members of the professional group with faculty status and membership in the faculty senate or council. However, a counselor's or librarian's rank, or official status, in the university is directly influenced by position classification concerns (for example, the number of people supervised) that grow out of the legacy of scientific management. In the case of Linden State I placed the librarians in the faculty, while the counselors were left in student affairs where they strove either to recast the style of decision-making or to become themselves members of the faculty and its senate.

In the closing chapter Jones designs an organizational strategy to cope with the challenges of "up-tight management." It should be emphasized that he would not claim to have discovered "the one best way" to organize a university. At best his is an honest effort to deal with the stresses and conflicts within his particular university in a manner that will promote continued organizational development—and his own continuance in his role.

In designing Linden State I debated with myself before choosing a setting in which the university had its own unique board (independent from a university system) in a legislatively dominated state. Ultimately I chose the setting I did for the purposes of simplicity in developing a narrative that would illustrate the particular points that I wished to make.

However, the decision to give Linden State an independent administration serving under its own governing board means that the stress between a central office and a local campus has been omitted from the narrative. Jones' brief encounter with the State Education Commission does not substitute adequately for the vigorous struggles that frequently characterize central office-local campus relations. I suspect that these struggles are often vigorous enough to make into battle cries the abstract concepts in public administration of "centralization" and "decentralization."

If I had selected a state in which the executive branch is dominant, I would have been required to add another layer to the chapter dealing with Linden State's budget. A state department of budget or finance would have played a significant role, but the legislature could not have been left out if there were to be any degree of realism in the narrative. I wish I had been able to discuss the orientations of state budget and management experts. In particular I wanted to discuss them as the heirs of scientific management but with a significant difference.

Unlike their predecessors, they seem to me to place little emphasis on the need for "unity of command." Instead, armed with new technologies and information systems, they focus on individual university subsystems as if the university were a machine that can be disassembled and rearranged at will in order to maximize efficiency and (above all) to save money.

Although Linden State is different from other universities, I believe that the forces described in the narrative are at work in different forms in many public universities and especially in those universities that would not be included among the well established research universities.

Turnover rates among university presidents indicate to me that there is much to the concept of "up-tight management," but I would be remiss if I did not also mention the satisfactions and joys that go with the position of a university president. We presidents are given the unique opportunity to interact with a wonderfully talented group of professionals. We go to their lectures, plays, and musical performances. We read their books and puzzle over their art forms. We are privileged to know young students who truly are the nation's future and older students who seek through the university answers to many of the same questions that bother us. We cheer at football games because we want to and we uniformly enjoy commencements. Besides which, we are constantly reminded by our colleagues that if our jobs were not difficult they could be done by our secretaries at a considerable savings.

In the narrative I consciously healed the wounds of the actors consistent with an organic view of the university as an interdependent body or community. When it is wounded, the university, like Jones, has the potential to heal itself and to continue its growth. Its stresses, I would argue, often can be the source of its advancement.

Throughout the book Jones exposes to us his many follies, but I also hope that he appears as a man who has the virtues of caring about his university, of reflecting upon his situation, and then of acting to seek his own and his university's fulfillment.

ABOUT THE AUTHOR

Like his fictional counterpart, Harold Haak has had ample opportunity to observe the inner workings of the university. He has been president of California State University, Fresno since February 1980, after serving for six years as the chancellor of the University of Colorado at Denver. He also held administrative posts as a vice president for academic affairs and as a school dean. Prior to entering university administration, he served as an officer of two faculty organizations and as an elected member of the Statewide Academic Senate of the California State University. Dr. Haak received his B.A. and M.A. degrees from the University of Wisconsin and Ph.D. in political science from Princeton University.